Exploring the Pacific

DISCOVERY & EXPLORATION

Exploring the Pacific

MARTHA VAIL

JOHN S. BOWMAN and MAURICE ISSERMAN
General Editors

Facts On File, Inc.

Exploring the Pacific

Facts On File, Inc.
132 West 31st Street
New York NY 10001

Library of Congress Cataloging-in-Publication Data

Exploring the Pacific / Martha Vail, John S. Bowman, and Maurice Isserman, general editors.
    p. cm. — (Discovery and exploration)
Includes bibliographical references and index.
ISBN 0-8160-5258-1 (alk. paper)
    1. Pacific Ocean—Disovery and exploration—Juvenile literature. 2. Explorers—Pacific area—Juvenile literature. I. Vail, Martha. II. Bowman, John Stewart, 1931– III. Isserman, Maurice. IV. Series.
DU19.E96 2005
919.04—dc22   2004006807

Facts On File books are available at special discounts when purchased in bulk quantities for businesses, associations, institutions, or sales promotions. Please call our Special Sales Department in New York at (212) 967-8800 or (800) 322-8755.

You can find Facts On File on the World Wide Web at
http://www.factsonfile.com

Text design by Erika K. Arroyo
Cover design by Pehrsson Design
Maps by Patricia Meschino and Dale Williams

Printed in the United States of America

VB FOF 10 9 8 7 6 5 4 3 2 1

This book is printed on acid-free paper.

Me ke aloha, Esther Handleman Vail

CONTENTS

Note on Photos

Many of the illustrations and photographs used in this book are old, historical images. The quality of the prints is not always up to current standards, as in some cases the originals are from old or poor-quality negatives or are damaged. The content of the illustrations, however, made their inclusion important despite problems in reproduction.

INTRODUCTION

 The words of explorer James Cook, "ambition leads me not only farther than any man has been before me, but as far as I think it is possible for men to go," are found in collections of quotations, on inspirational posters, and somewhere in most books about Cook. The real nature of Cook's greatness is revealed when the January 30, 1774, entry from his journal continues. Cook's ships, the *Resolution* and the *Adventure*, had sailed far below the Antarctic Circle. At 71° south latitude a wall of ice forced Cook to turn his ships around. Cook "was not sorry at meeting with this interruption as it in some measure relieved us from the dangers and hardship, inseparable with the Navigation of the Polar Region."

Cook, considered by many to be the greatest explorer of the Pacific—and perhaps of any region on Earth—was no coward. His genius was in calculating the measure of danger and hardship that his men and ships could endure to expand the limits of the known world. The history of exploration in the Pacific is one of courage, of risk, of happy accident. But it is also one of misery beyond words, cruelty, and tragedy. It is not the story of men and ships, even of brave men like Cook and gallant ships like the *Resolution*. Rather, exploration of the

Pacific has been a vast mirror of the world's history, from the earliest ocean voyaging to the trade routes that link the West and the East to this day.

Explorers of the Pacific had their most important achievements in expanding geographical knowledge. The maps, charts, paintings, and reports generated during voyages of discovery document a monumental increase in human understanding. Polynesian voyagers crafted stick charts to guide traders and settlers from one island to another lying far beyond the horizon. In 1607, Spanish explorer Luiz Vaez de Torres charted a course through the channel between Australia and New Guinea—now called Torres Strait—still used by supertankers navigating the strait that bears his name. As philosopher John Locke wrote in a 1704 collection about voyages of discovery, "the Relation of one traveller is an Incentive to stir up another to imitate him. . . ." Exploration was fundamentally path breaking, an opening of new places to following generations of traders, soldiers, scientists, settlers, and tourists.

Much of the exploration of the Pacific was significant for what was *not* discovered. In the second century A.D., Egyptian geographer Ptolemy argued that a huge landmass must exist in the Southern Hemisphere. A thousand years later merchant Marco Polo speculated that this great continent, rich in gold and populated by millions of souls, awaited European ships venturing beyond the fabled Spice Islands. Five hundred years of exploration was driven by the quest for this so-called Terra Australis Incognita. The possibility that a Northwest Passage to the Pacific existed on the American continent tantalized European scholars, politicians, and explorers for centuries. In searching for the passage, explorers from France, Spain, Russia, England, and the United States documented the west coast of North America and ventured into the Arctic.

Each ship that ventured into the Pacific around the Cape of Good Hope, through the Strait of Magellan, or around Cape Horn carried the hope and ambitions of its nation. The Pacific, perhaps even more than the Americas or Africa, became the playing board for a global game of imperial chess. Early expeditions aimed to wrestle control of the spice trade from Arab hands and to convert millions to Christianity. By the 17th century the nations of Europe sent their ships to gain markets for all sorts of goods. In the 18th and 19th centuries, expeditions sailed to demonstrate scientific or technological superiority, to establish colonies, and to annex strategic military positions. Remote from the islands of the Pacific, struggles for domination of the European continent, such as the War of the Spanish Succession, profoundly affected the destiny of island peoples. By the 20th century, only the most remote and inhospitable islands were free from American, European, or South American colonial administration.

Both a product and an object of exploration, scientific discovery occurs as a persistent theme in the exploration of the Pacific. Even before expeditions undertook explicitly scientific missions in the 18th century, ships'

logs and sailors' journals were full of observations about the natural world. Gentleman-sailor Francisco Antonio Pigafetta, whose journal contains the best contemporary account of Ferdinand Magellan's circumnavigation, observed the behavior of the fish he saw in mid-ocean: "There are three sorts of fish in this ocean a cubit or more in length. . . . These follow and hunt another kind of fish which flies and which we called Colondriny [sea swallow]." Only through the application of known theories and experimentation on his ships was Cook able to devise a method for preventing scurvy that saved thousands of lives. Scientists accompanying Cook, Louis-Antoine de Bougainville, and George Vancouver made major contributions in the fields of astronomy, navigation, botany, and zoology. In the late 19th century the Pacific incubated an entirely new field of science—oceanography—which continues to drive exploration of its darkest depths.

Explorers introduced newfound lands to all sorts of change and exchange. Polynesian rafts brought sweet potatoes, breadfruit trees, and pigs as well as settlers to far-flung islands. Recent work by anthropologists and archaeologists such as Patrick Kirch traces the expansion of human settlement in the Pacific by documenting human remains, plants, and domesticated animals. Geneticists such as Anne Gibbons have suggested that distinctions between Melanesian, Micronesian, and Polynesian peoples are artificial. Rather than describing real racial differences, the terms should be understood as broad definitions of geographic regions and cultural groups. Biological change and exchange marked the European exploration of the Pacific as well. Some change was one-sided and devastating, as disease decimated the populations of many islands. Some exchange was reciprocal. When explorer Samuel Wallis planted English cherry trees on Tahiti in 1767, he marked the Pacific landscape with the biology of Europe. When botanist David Nelson brought plants from the Pacific to the Royal Botanic Gardens in 1780, the flora of the Pacific changed the English landscape.

Cultural change and exchange are equally important in the history of Pacific exploration. Strikingly similar patterns can be found on pottery, carving, and tattoos throughout the Pacific, indicating vast and ancient networks of trade and settlement. Linguistic and religious similarities speak to such connections as well. Europeans entered this connected, yet diverse, world of the Pacific with a worldview that characterized its people as "savages" in need of civilizing and "heathens" in need of christianizing. By the 18th century, European attitudes about native peoples shifted somewhat. Islanders were seen as living in a perfect state of nature, and even those Pacific peoples who traveled to Europe were exhibited as "noble savages."

James Cook was asked that his first expedition record the "Features, Complection [sic], Dress, Habitations, Food, Weapons" of the islanders he met and to document "Religion, Morals Order, Government, Distinctions of Power, Police" on the islands. Clearly, Europeans no longer thought islanders lacked cultural traditions and institutions, and interest in learning more about them grew. As historian Anne Salmond demonstrates in *The Trial of the Cannibal Dog,* European interest in Pacific cultures did not necessarily result in mutual understanding. Ethnographic observations by 18th- and 19th-century expedition scientists were accompanied by illustrations of Pacific peoples and their environments created by expedition artists. Together, these resources provide some idea of life in both the northern and southern regions of the Pacific at a moment when contact with Western culture, technology, and colonialism introduced massive and permanent change. The recent debate between scholars Marshall Sahlins and Gananath Obeyesekere over Hawaiian interpretations of James Cook's death reflects the importance of including native Pacific sources in this ethnographic portrait.

The French philosopher Denis Diderot referred to the Pacific as an "ocean of fantasy." Just as Polynesians repeated stories about semidivine ancestors who fished up islands, Europeans created an imaginary sea in which fiction and fact intertwined. Thomas More's *Utopia,* Edmund Spenser's *Faerie Queene,* and Jonathan Swift's *Gulliver's Travels* all had Pacific landscapes, even before much was known about the South Seas. Accounts by explorers and travelers sold widely in Europe through the early 20th century, as did works of fiction by writers such as Robert Louis Stevenson and Herman Melville. Even today, dreams of tropical paradise are inspired by articles in glossy travel magazines and by instructional Web sites for Westerners yearning to abandon civilized life for a remote Pacific utopia. The scholar Jonathan Lamb, who writes extensively and with careful scholarship about cultural changes and exchanges incited by Pacific exploration, describes Europeans as genuinely "at sea" in the Pacific. If trade, religion, science, and empire create neat narratives and straightforward storylines about European expansion into the Pacific, then the world of literature captures the ambivalent encounter between ships and islands.

1

"TIDE BEATING HEART OF THE EARTH"

 On July 30, 1768, the man in charge of all British naval affairs, Edward Hawk, First Lord of the Admiralty, delivered to First Lieutenant James Cook of the Royal Navy two sets of orders labeled "secret." Cook, an extraordinary sailor of ordinary origins, had been given command of His Majesty's Ship *Endeavour* two months earlier and had been instructed to prepare the 105-foot long, 368-ton ship with its crew of 94 men for a voyage to the Pacific Ocean.

Europeans had first gazed on Pacific waters 250 years earlier. Portuguese, English, Spanish, French, and Dutch ships had wandered the past two centuries over the broad reaches of the world's largest body of water. Yet uncounted islands, peoples, species, and continents—both real and imagined—lay tantalizingly over the sparkling blue horizon. Cook's ambition was to number the wonders of the vast Pacific Ocean that Herman Melville, the author of *Moby Dick,* called the "tide beating heart of the Earth."

THE *ENDEAVOUR*'S FIRST ORDERS:
The Transit of Venus

The first set of orders, as expected, directed Cook to sail HMS *Endeavour* to Tahiti. There, expedition scientists would establish an observatory to study the passage of the planet Venus across the sun, an event that occurs so rarely that only five have been observed since 1639. Accurate observations would make it possible to measure Earth's distance from the sun. This measurement, known as the "astronomical unit," was essential in understanding the size of the universe. Scientists all over Europe eagerly anticipated the event.

English naturalist John Ellis described the equipment of the *Endeavour* in a letter to Swedish scientist Carl Linneaus several days before the expedition's departure: "No people ever went to sea better fitted out for the purpose of Natural History, nor more elegantly." Indeed, Cook's ship was a floating laboratory.

1

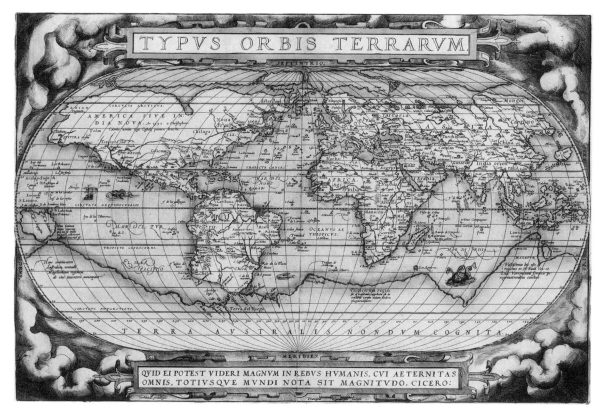

TYPVS ORBIS TERRARVM

QVID EI POTEST VIDERI MAGNVM IN REBVS HVMANIS, CVI AETERNITAS
OMNIS, TOTIVSQVE MVNDI NOTA SIT MAGNITVDO. CICERO:

Dutch geographer Abraham Ortelius published this map of the world in his 1570 *Theatrum Orbis Terrarum,* or *Theater of the World,* which contained 70 maps and is one of the earliest atlases. Much was still unknown about the Pacific Ocean at the time. *(Library of Congress, Geography and Maps Division)*

Its crew included astronomers, artists, and biologists. Cook himself was an accomplished, self-taught mathematician. The *Endeavour* was specially equipped with facilities to process and store all sorts of biological specimens, and its scientists recorded in great detail each new natural phenomenon encountered during the voyage.

THE *ENDEAVOUR*'S SECOND ORDERS:
The Great Southern Continent

Early Greek geographers, firmly believing that the Earth was round, thought that the Southern Hemisphere was mostly ocean. Second-century A.D. Egyptian geographer Ptolemy—best known for his logical demonstration of the Earth's sphericity—argued that a large landmass existed to the south of Africa. By the 16th century cartographers such as Gerardius Mercator theorized that the Southern Hemisphere must contain a very large continent, or else the Earth would be in danger of toppling over. Moreover, powerful religious and political leaders believed such a vast land must contain thousands of souls who needed the salvation offered only through Christianity. Inca tales passed to Spanish explorers told of fabulously rich lands beyond South America, perhaps the source of King Solomon's gold.

Proof of the existence of Terra Australis Incognita eluded explorers of the Pacific for centuries, and its discovery remained a glittering prize. The English writer Jonathan Swift, who set the fantasy lands—including Lilliput, Brobdingnag, and Balnibarbi—of *Gulliver's Travels* in the Pacific, made fun of the obsession with the Great Southern Continent in his 1704 essay, *Project for the Universal Benefit of Mankind:*

> The author, having laboured so long, and done so much to serve and instruct the public, without any advantage to himself has at last thought of a project, which will tend to the benefit of mankind, and produce a handsome revenue to the author. He intends to print by subscription, in 96 large volumes in *folio* an exact description of *Terra Australis incognita* collected with great care and pains from 999 learned and pious authors, of undoubted veracity.

In 1767, Alexander Dalrymple, a hydrographer who made maps and charts for the English East India Company, published *An Account of the Discoveries Made in the South Pacific Ocean Previous to 1764*. Dalrymple, widely regarded as the leading expert on the Pacific, argued, "A continent is wanted on the south . . . to counterpoise the land on the north and to maintain the equilibrium necessary for the earth's motion." Dalrymple—who would be the leading candidate for the command of the Transit of Venus expedition, but was disqualified because he was a civilian—further stated that the Great Southern Continent lay approximately at 40 degrees latitude south, extended from east to west more than 5,300 miles, and had a population of 50 million.

Such a vast, treasure-filled land would reward the European nation that could lay claim to it first in the global race to acquire overseas territories. England's great rival, France, was anxious to acquire Terra Australis Incognita for its own empire. Thus, the Transit of Venus was simply a convenient cover for the second, more important phase of the *Endeavour*'s voyage.

The Admiralty had instructed Cook not to open the second set of orders until the Transit of Venus had been duly calculated. As the *Endeavour* sailed from Tahiti's Matavai Bay on

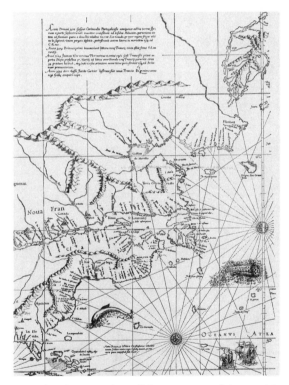

Gerardus Mercator's well-known map of the world was first published in 1569. In the portion shown here, the cartographer's use of what would become known as Mercator projection, in which longitude is drawn as parallel lines meeting latitudinal lines at right angles, is evident. *(Library of Congress, Prints and Photographs Division [LC-USZ62-92883])*

August 9, 1769, Cook opened his orders. The *Endeavour* was to sail to the south as far as 40 degrees latitude in search of the southern continent. If the continent remained hidden, Cook was to sail west to New Zealand and to "explore as much of the Coast as the Condition of the Bark, the health of her Crew, and the State of Your Provisions will admit of." The task was as spectacular and unlimited as Cook's own ambition.

THE FIRST PACIFIC EXPLORERS

The Pacific is the largest of Earth's five oceans. Encompassing the South and East China Seas, the Sea of Japan, and the Bering Sea, the Pacific covers 64,186,000 square miles. The Pacific is 15 times larger than the United States and represents 28 percent of the Earth's surface. The ocean's northernmost reaches extend to the Kamchatka Peninsula in western Russia and to the Aleutian island chain in Alaska. Mount Cook, in New Zealand, is the highest elevation in the Pacific region, at 12,316 feet. The Mariana Trench, in the western Pacific, descending 35,806 feet, is the world's deepest ocean trench.

The theory of plate tectonics identifies seven large plates, and many smaller ones, that make up the Earth's crust. These plates shift about two inches a year, forming and reforming continents and oceans over millions of years. Several major plates—the Pacific, Nazca, Cocos, Philippine, Indo-Australian, and Antarctic—lie under the Pacific Ocean, constantly bumping against each other. The resulting seismic activity is frequent and sometimes calamitous in the northwest part of the ocean and along the ocean's shores, giving the Pacific Rim its nickname, Ring of Fire. In 1886 the explosion of Krakatoa volcano between Sumatra and Java resulted in the deaths of 36,000 people. These plates also account for the fact that the southern, eastern, and central parts of the ocean are geologically stable and contain few islands. Early explorers could sail in these regions for two months without sighting land.

Within the enormous area of the Pacific lies a surprisingly small amount of land, all of it encompassing more than 7,500 islands. Many islands are the tops of extinct volcanoes, while others are atolls, islands surrounded by coral reefs. And some islands, those characterized by craggy, cliff-lined coasts, are summits of submerged basaltic rock mountains. Enormous islands such as New Guinea and the north and south islands of New Zealand were once thought by Europeans to be the Great Southern Continent. Many Pacific islands are too small or too climactically hostile to support human life. Some islands in the Pacific are disappearing as the ocean's waters swell with melting polar ice caps. Scientists believe

This early 20th-century photograph of the beautiful natural harbor at Pago Pago on Tutuila, Samoa, shows a stereotypical tropical paradise. *(Library of Congress, Prints and Photographs Division [LC-USZ62-105590])*

that Funafuti, the main island of the Tuvalu group, will return to the ocean within 50 years. Tepuka Savilivili, its neighbor, has already disappeared.

Two main currents govern the waters of the Pacific Ocean. In the northern Pacific a clockwise system of warm currents is present. In the southern Pacific a counterclockwise, cool current circulates. Throughout much of the Pacific the climate is tropical, warm, and humid. In the far northern and southern Pacific extreme cold, ice, and winds presented challenges to generations of explorers.

ORIGINS OF PACIFIC PEOPLES

Although the Pacific Ocean is inhabited by .01 percent of the Earth's population, its people speak one-third of the world's languages. More than 700 different languages have been identified in New Guinea. New Guinea is also the most populous island, with 5 million inhabitants. The smallest island population, 47, can be found on remote Pitcairn Island. The demographic regions of the Pacific are the Northern Pacific, Melanesia, Micronesia, and Polynesia.

Although scientists believe the Pacific peoples have common roots in Asia, millennia of migration, immigration, trade, and contact with European cultures have resulted in a dazzling array of cultures in the Pacific.

Asian nomads moved into Siberia about 40,000 years ago. About 15,000 years ago some of their descendants moved across the Bering Strait, then a land bridge, into the Aleutian Islands and farther to coastal Alaska. Siberian and Alaskan Pacific people shared a culture for thousands of years. When Siberians developed reindeer breeding and metal work, about 2,000 years ago, these culture groups, such as the Chukchi and Karyak, became quite different from their near neighbors across the Bering Strait. These cultures developed into distinct traditions and ways of life

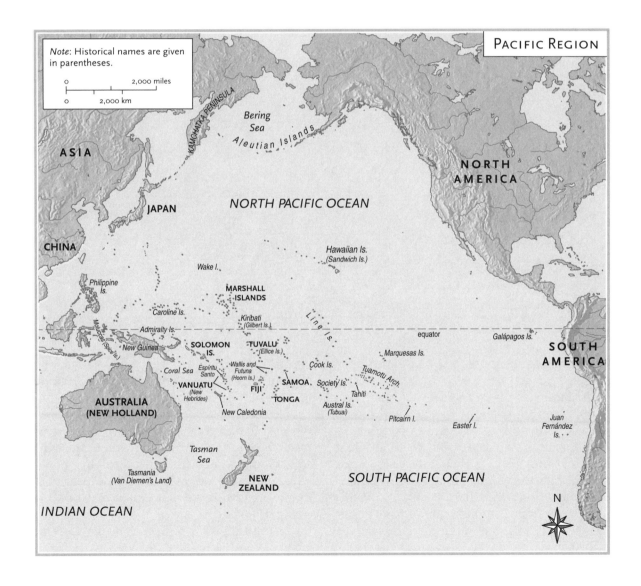

PACIFIC REGION

Note: Historical names are given in parentheses.

0 — 2,000 miles
0 — 2,000 km

KAMCHATKA PENINSULA

Bering Sea

Aleutian Islands

ASIA

JAPAN

NORTH PACIFIC OCEAN

NORTH AMERICA

CHINA

Hawaiian Is. (Sandwich Is.)

Wake I.

Philippine Is.

MARSHALL ISLANDS

Caroline Is.

Kiribati (Gilbert Is.)

Line Is.

Admiralty Is.

Moluccas (Spice Is.)

New Guinea

SOLOMON IS.

TUVALU (Ellice Is.)

equator

Galápagos Is.

SOUTH AMERICA

Marquesas Is.

Coral Sea

Espíritu Santo

Wallis and Futuna (Hoorn Is.)

Cook Is.

Tuamotu Arch.

VANUATU (New Hebrides)

FIJI

SAMOA

Society Is.

Tahiti

TONGA

Austral Is. (Tubuai)

AUSTRALIA (NEW HOLLAND)

New Caledonia

Pitcairn I.

Easter I.

Juan Fernández Is.

Tasman Sea

Tasmania (Van Diemen's Land)

NEW ZEALAND

SOUTH PACIFIC OCEAN

INDIAN OCEAN

N

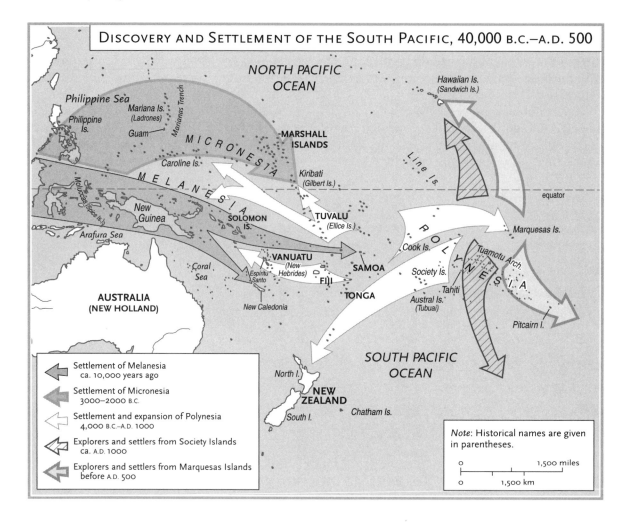

DISCOVERY AND SETTLEMENT OF THE SOUTH PACIFIC, 40,000 B.C.–A.D. 500

Legend:

- Settlement of Melanesia ca. 10,000 years ago
- Settlement of Micronesia 3000–2000 B.C.
- Settlement and expansion of Polynesia 4,000 B.C.–A.D. 1000
- Explorers and settlers from Society Islands ca. A.D. 1000
- Explorers and settlers from Marquesas Islands before A.D. 500

Note: Historical names are given in parentheses.

0   1,500 miles
0   1,500 km

among the Inuit, Inupiat, Yupik, and Alutiiq peoples.

Beginning as many as 50,000 years ago, people from Southeast Asia settled in the large islands north of Australia. These people also had a common ancestry with the aboriginal culture of Australia. For millennia New Guinea and the Solomon Islands were the only inhabited islands in the southern Pacific. Archaeologists have found human remains from about 25,000 years ago and stone tools more than 20,000 years old in New Guinea. The 19th-century French explorer Jules-Sébastien-César Dumont d'Urville called these islands Melanesia. He devised the term from the Greek words *mela* ("black"), because the people of this region are very dark-skinned, and *nesos* ("islands"). From the Solomons and New Guinea, joined by Austronesian people who may have originated in Taiwan, settlement spread as far as New Caledonia and Vanuatu by 5000 B.C.

Around 2000 B.C., Micronesia ("small islands") was inhabited through a dynamic process of voyage, settlement, conquest, and colonization by migrants from Indonesia, the Philippines, and Melanesia. Fairer skinned than the Melanesians, and possessing a broad diversity of distinct cultures, the peoples of Micronesia live in a region of more than 2,500 islands, including the Caroline, Marshall, and Northern Marianas island groups. Just before the beginning of European voyages in the region, in the 15th century, a man-made island, Lelu, with an extensive walled compound was built on the island of Kosrae. The ruins at Lelu indicate that precontact Melanesian culture was at once egalitarian and competitive.

Earlier, about 5,000 years ago (circa 3000 B.C.), the culture that archaeologists and anthropologists believe to be the ancestor of the peoples of Polynesia ("many islands") was spreading from Melanesia. This culture, known as *Lapita,* takes its name from a site in New Caledonia where archaeologists unearthed many examples of a distinctive form of pottery. Before firing, the potter stamped large ceramic vessels with a tool that looked like a comb, incising a linear pattern. One simple design was combined with others to create complicated patterns. Designs found on pottery from Lapita are also found on *tapa* (bark cloth) textiles throughout the western Pacific, as well as in traditional Samoan tattoos and Tongan war clubs. Tracing the spread of Lapita design elements, scientists have been able to better understand the exploration and settlement patterns of the ancient people of Polynesia.

Probably created in the 1920s or 1930s, this image of Fiji, composed of more than 840 islands, presents a lush and vibrant environment. Its original inhabitants included Melanesian and Polynesian peoples. *(National Archives of Canada)*

By 300 B.C. voyagers from Samoa and Tonga had discovered and settled the Cook, Society, Tuamoto, and Marquesas island groups. Within 800 years, or by about A.D. 400, Polynesian people lived as far into the Pacific as Easter Island and the Hawaiian Islands. Scholars speculate that the Hawaiian people have two ancestral homes in Polynesia. Because the languages of Hawaii and the Marquesas possess a 56 percent similarity, anthropologists conclude that the first settlers voyaged from the Marquesas. A later wave of immigrants arrived from the Society Islands around A.D. 1000. At the same time, explorers from the Cook or Society Islands reached and inhabited Aotearoa (New Zealand), and the perimeters of the Polynesian triangle were completed.

POLYNESIAN VOYAGING

The folklore of Polynesia is a rich source for historians and anthropologists seeking to understand the remarkable cultural similarities among its far-flung people. A Tahitian legend tells of ancient explorer Tafa'i, the son of a human man and goddess of the underworld Hina-tahutahu. Tafa'i fished for islands. First he fished up the islands of the Tuamotu group and then sailed off to the north. There he found a chain of undersea islands, hauled up the first and named it *Aihi,* or Hawaii, and fished up the rest of the Hawaiian islands. Tafa'i then sailed back to Tahiti to fetch settlers for the new islands. When the settlers followed Tafa'i to Hawaii, they brought with them their plants, their chiefs, and their gods.

Polynesians sought to find new lands with a minimal risk of death at sea. Sailing against the wind to the East as far as their supplies would carry them, which could be as long as six or seven weeks on the larger ships, the explorers would venture out into the ocean.

When their provisions ran low they would return home quickly, with the wind behind them. Settlers would follow the explorers' route, heading for the newly discovered lands. The migrants brought food-bearing plants and livestock, since most of the newly discovered islands had neither. When population pressures, war, or simple curiosity reached

This engraving by John Webber, an artist on James Cook's third voyage, shows two explorers' ships (on the right) and some canoes in the Society Islands. *(Library of Congress, Prints and Photographs Division [LC-USZ62-102092])*

critical mass on the new home island, the process of discovery and settlement would be repeated.

Some Polynesian exploration may have been accidental, as fishermen followed migrating schools of fish or trading expeditions were blown off course. In 1947, Norwegian anthropologist Thor Heyerdahl suggested another explanation for Polynesian origin and exploration. Setting off from the coast of Peru in the balsawood raft *Kon-Tiki,* Heyerdahl traveled 4,000 miles in 100 days and landed in the Tuamotu Archipelago. He wanted to prove it possible that the ancient Polynesians actually originated in South America. Dramatic and courageous as Heyerdahl's experiment

Early Pacific Navigation

The early Pacific navigators made voyages over vast reaches of the ocean, journeys that seem unfathomable without navigational instruments like the compass. Yet ancient peoples were able to travel as far as from Tahiti to Hawaii, conquering the doldrums, a band of calm waters around the equator. Early navigators employed many techniques to find their way in the Pacific. All navigation depended on highly developed senses of sight, smell, touch, hearing, and the passage of time. Explorers constantly observed the patterns of the waves, swells, and winds. A chant from the Tuamotu archipelago honored and personified the winds:

> *Oh West Wind!*
> *You dwell in the deep caverns*
> *of the realm of night;*
> *Sharp is your chilly breath*
> *Coming from the ocean wastes, beyond the setting sun,*
> *where storm clouds gather.*

Sightings of particular species of fish might mean land was near, as would the appearance of floating vegetation. Boats would follow the path of birds returning to land after hunting at sea for fish. Sailors looked for banks of clouds, clustering over an island. A form of dead reckoning, in which sailors memorized the direction traveled and the distance covered until land was reached, also guided ships across open sea.

Early Polynesian navigators possessed deep knowledge of astronomy. One method identified the "top star" for a particular island. When the star Sirius was directly above the voyagers' heads, they knew they were in the latitude of Tahiti. In another method, sailors would chart their course by dividing the horizon into 16 sections, using the points of the rising and setting sun as cardinal points. Later navigators devised stick charts, with sticks representing the direction of ocean currents, and shells threaded on the sticks to indicate known islands. Master navigators, such as the Tahitian *fa'atere,* were specially honored in Pacific island cultures. In the 17th century, European explorers would depend on the greater knowledge of these masters as they ventured through the southern Pacific.

was, subsequent archaeological and anthropological work, such as the tracing of Lapita patterns, confirms that Polynesia was settled from west to east. Recent experimental voyages undertaken by the Polynesian Voyaging Society in recreations of ancient Polynesian sailing ships have demonstrated that open ocean journeys as long as from Tahiti to Hawaii would have been possible before the fifth century A.D. By contrast, Viking ships did not reach the shores of North America until the 10th century.

The ships of the first Pacific explorers were either canoes dug out of tree trunks or barges made of planks fastened together with coconut fiber ropes. *Vaa,* small paddled fishing boats, were about 15 feet long. Used in deep-sea fishing or traveling between neighboring islands, a 25- to 35-foot-long *vaa taie* had an outrigger for added stability, and sails for greater speed. *Pahi,* ships intended for long distances, were constructed of two canoes connected by crossbeams on which a platform was built that supported two masts. The platform also carried people and cargo. The boats were paddled in calm seas. When the wind rose, sails fashioned of woven leaves were raised. These sailboats were durable— after all, the distance from Tahiti to Hawaii is 2,000 miles. They were often very large,

between 60 and 100 feet long. Captain James Cook measured one Tahitian canoe at three feet longer than his ship, the *Endeavour.* And they were fast. One of Cook's sailors estimated that a canoe from Tonga could sail "three miles to our two."

As the islands of Polynesia were settled, their inhabitants would travel back and forth among them. This two-way voyaging served many purposes. Islanders would trade goods unique to one island with a neighbor. An ancient story in Rarotonga tells about a man with a wife named Pepe-iu who traveled to Hiva-oa, in the Marquesas, to import breadfruit trees. Pigs would be raised for trade with distant islands. Wars and feuds propelled warriors to invade or raid other islands. Family quarrels could inspire family members to

John Webber's engraving shows an inland view of Kauai, one of the islands of Hawaii, featuring inhabitants and their dwellings. James Cook explored the islands of Hawaii in 1778. *(Library of Congress, Prints and Photographs Division [LC-USZ62-102234])*

move to or sojourn on another island. A Hawaiian legend tells of the brothers Pa'ao and Lonopele, who both lived on the island of Ra'iatea and who fought and killed one another's sons. To end the feud, Pa'ao left Ra'iatea and settled in Hawaii. Because islands were often settled by only two or three families, men and women would choose mates from a different island. Some two-way voyaging had a religious purpose. The bodies of members of early generations on a newly settled island would be returned to the home island for burial. If an offspring island failed to develop adequate leadership, *mana* (spiritual power) would be acquired by inviting a person of the noble class on the home island to emigrate. Similarly, gods could be brought from one island to another.

Some voyaging may have been simply for a love of adventure or out of a sense of curiosity about what lay beyond the horizon. Another Polynesian folktale relates the story of the brother and sister Ru and Hina. Ru and Hina circumnavigated the Earth in their canoe *Te-apori,* searching for new islands. When they had discovered all the islands on Earth, Hina's thirst for exploration was unquenched, so she sailed *Te-apori* over the horizon to the moon. Hina became the Polynesian version of the Man (or, in this case, Woman) in the Moon.

Art of the Pacific Peoples

For Pacific peoples, as for all cultures, art speaks to and from myths, values, and traditions. Artists were, and are, given special status in Pacific communities. In Hawaii a piece of *tapa* (bark cloth) is considered to be imbued with the *mana* (spiritual power) of its maker, and *tapa* is frequently used in life cycle and religious ceremonies. Early European explorers collected many artifacts as they sailed the Pacific, and classically trained European artists traveling with voyages of discovery documented art throughout the Pacific. Nineteenth-century missionaries understood the spiritual significance of much Pacific art and feared that such art would stand in the way of people accepting Christianity. Missionaries often attempted to ban its production, and countless artifacts were destroyed.

One of the most well-known Pacific art forms is tattooing. The word *tattoo* means "striking continuously" in Tahitian. James Cook was the first European to record tattoos, writing in his diary, "they print signs on people's body and call this tattow." Tattoos were created with a sharp instrument of bone, shell, or animal tooth tapped with a small mallet. An indelible pigment made from ashes mixed with coconut oil was applied to various body parts, very often the buttocks and sometimes even the tongue. Master artists followed strict traditions and were trained in a lengthy apprenticeship. Tattoos represented a person's identity, rank, and clan membership. Tattoos were also considered protection against malevolent spirits and were incorporated in coming-of-age ceremonies. Tattoo patterns in the Pacific include geometric figures, patterns emulating natural forms, and representations of animals.

As populations stabilized, food crops were established, and family connections with other islands were forgotten, so the need for two-way voyaging diminished. The last trips from Hawaii to Tahiti probably took place in the 14th century. Not until the European expeditions of the 18th century employed or coerced Polynesians to guide them through the Pacific would long ocean voyages reenter Polynesian life.

Because people ranging out through the Pacific from Melanesia settled the islands of Polynesia, and because travel and commerce had been common, the cultures on islands thousands of miles apart were often quite similar. James Cook, whose explorations took him to many Polynesian islands, wondered at these similarities and considered the Polynesians one people. Cook wrote, "I find such an affinity in the Language, Manner, and Custom of the different Islanders that I am led to believe that they all had one Origin." Linguistic similarities are common in Polynesia. For example, the tradition of searching for islands is called *imi fenua* in the Marquesas and *imi honua* in Hawaii. Early European visitors noted a preference on many islands for dwellings scattered throughout an island rather than clustered in villages. Similarly, work and ritual responsibilities were organized through *ohana,* or extended family networks, rather than by a centralized leadership or hierarchy.

The same, or very similar, myths about creation, gods, and human origins were found on islands distant from one another. Folktales from a number of islands describe a mythic island, Kahiki, as the place where all people originated. The concept of *tapu,* which has come into the English language as *taboo,* seems to have been a guiding principle on many islands. *Tapu,* or *kapu* in Hawaiian, was used to denote something sacred. It did not mean "forbidden," as Europeans thought, but designated something that could be contaminated by contact with unauthorized people or by incorrect handling. *Tapu* was often connected to the *alii,* who were leaders or nobility. *Alii* status was hereditary on many islands, and *alii* served as liaisons between the people and the most powerful gods. On some islands, including Hawaii, whose last monarch was Queen Liliuokalani, *alii* could be female.

THE SEVEN VOYAGES OF ZHENG HE

About the same time that Polynesians stopped making two-way voyages between islands, Chinese ships appeared in the Pacific. In the early 15th century, Chinese commander Zheng He (Cheng Ho) conducted a series of seven expeditions that took him from China to as far as Arabia. Zheng He commanded as many as 27,000 men and 317 ships during voyages occurring between 1405 and 1435. One of his expeditions had a fleet of 63 ships sailing together. Most were junks, some capable of carrying a crew of a thousand, and most five times larger than the caravels the Portuguese would sail into the Indian Ocean later that century.

In the mid-14th century Chinese rebels rose up against the Mongol conquerors who had controlled China for more than a hundred years. By 1382 all of China was ruled by the Ming dynasty. With Mongols still powerful to the west, the Chinese turned to the sea to begin an empire and began to build a navy. Forests were planted near the new capital of Nanjing (Nanking) to supply the timber and varnish needed to build ships. Shipyards were constructed. Schools for interpreters, navigators, and mapmakers were established. Sailors were trained in the use of the compass, which was known as the "south pointing spoon" and also used as a fortune-telling tool.

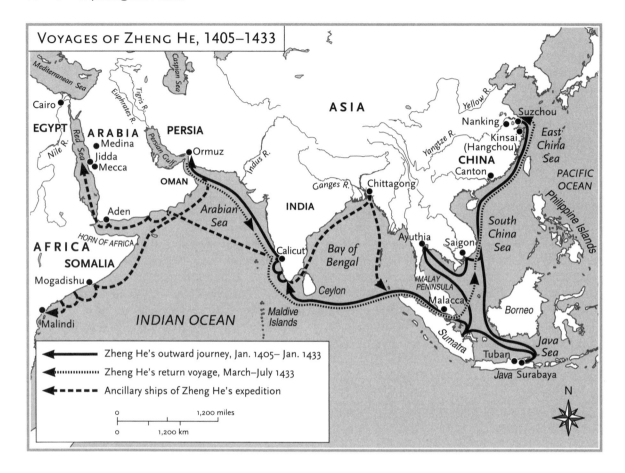

In 1405, Ming emperor Cheng Tsu (Ch'eng Tsu, known also as the Yongle [Yung-lo] Emperor) sent Zheng He to gather information about the lands bordering the Pacific and Indian Oceans. A monument celebrating Zheng He in his native province was erected during his lifetime. It records the emperor's assignment to Zheng He to explore "the countries beyond the horizon, all the way to the ends of the earth." From Nanjing in northeastern China, Zheng He and his ships sailed along the Pacific coast of China, and then to India, where the expedition anchored off Calicut. Returning to China, Zheng He sailed through the Straits of Malacca and encoun-

tered the islands of Java and Sumatra. He established a base at the Straits of Malacca that served as a provisioning spot for his future voyages. The base also contained a warehouse for goods, such as porcelains and silks, that the Chinese wished to trade with foreign nations and for tribute given to Zheng He on his visits to faraway ports.

Zheng He would be sent on six more expeditions to explore, to trade, to collect taxes from China's colonies, and to demonstrate Chinese power. Each expedition was provisioned with enough rice and preserved foods to feed the crew for months before they had to resort to "barbarian" foods in port. Large containers of dirt were brought on board to make gardens that would provide fresh vegetables and fruits. Zheng He's crews included diplomats, doctors, shipwrights, and scribes, who recorded the voyages. Buddhist monks and Muslim *imams* (priests) served as diplomats to foreign powers.

Zheng He's ships crossed the Arabian Sea to explore the Persian Gulf. He made a pilgrimage to Mecca and visited Muhammad's tomb in Medina. On one of Zheng He's expeditions Chinese ships reached Somalia on the eastern coast of Africa. It is possible that one of Zheng He's voyages took him to the northern coast of Australia two centuries before European explorers reached its shores. The Chinese ships traded extensively and brought back medicines, spices, gems, pearls, and exotic animals.

They also brought back important information about new lands, potential trading partners, political alliances, and new shipping routes. Zheng He wrote of his adventures, "We have . . . beheld in the ocean huge waves like mountains rising sky-high, and we have set eyes on barbarian regions far away hidden in a blue transparency of light vapors, while our sails, loftily unfurled like clouds, day and night continued their course rapid like that of a star, traversing the savage waves as if we were treading a public thoroughfare."

Zheng He died on his seventh voyage, in 1435. After the greatest period of sea voyaging the world had known, the Chinese empire turned to consolidating its control over its inland territories and to protecting its borders from invasions by the Mongols' successors, the Tartars. No further expeditions were organized, and the huge oceangoing ships were destroyed.

3

EUROPEANS ENCOUNTER THE PACIFIC, FROM EAST AND WEST

 For Europeans, as for Polynesian voyagers and Chinese emperors, the waters and islands of the Pacific offered fantastic opportunities for wealth and power. Europeans felt the promise of the Pacific before they even saw the ocean or had a name for it. By the 13th century, the Italian city-states of Genoa and Venice had grown rich from trading with the East. Commerce connected Italian traders to a great land and sea network stretching from the Spice Islands and China to the important trading centers of Cairo and Constantinople. Catholic merchants from Italy joined the Hindus, Buddhists, and Muslims of the Middle and Far East in moving treasures across half the globe. Genoa and Venice together held a virtual monopoly on the importation of luxury goods—dyes, spices, silks, ivory, pearls, gold, and porcelains—into Europe, and thus controlled its economy.

In 1271, Italian merchant Marco Polo left Italy with his father, Nicolò, and his uncle Maffeo. The Polos traveled through the Middle East, China, and Southeast Asia for more than 20 years. Returning to Venice in 1295, Polo soon published *Description of the World*, also known as *The Travels of Marco Polo*. His account, which came to be called *Il Milione* by those who thought it contained a million lies, became one of the most popular books in Europe. In it Polo told of his journeys in China and as far south as Sumatra, and of lands of powerful rulers, massive elephants, and fabulous amounts of gold. Polo was probably describing Thailand or the Malay Peninsula. His *Travels* also included many tales of lands he did not actually visit during his 20-year odyssey. One of these described a great land south of Java, which he called Locach. The name was corrupted to Lubach and then, possibly by the cartographer Gerardus Mercator, to Beach. In the minds of Europeans, "Beach" became identified with the Great Southern Continent, a source of untold wealth and perhaps the location of the biblical King Solomon's gold mines.

The Spice Trade

The East has long been legendary as the source of spices, rich fabrics, and precious gems. In the Bible, Ezekiel 27:22 reads: "The traffickers of Sheba and Raamah, they were thy traffickers; they traded for thy wares with chief of all spices, and with all precious stones, and gold." From biblical times, or even earlier according to some archaeological evidence, Arab peoples served as traders of spices, silks, and precious minerals. As Islam spread through the Middle East and Southeast Asia, so did Arab control of the spice trade. Careful to hide the origins of their goods in the Spice Islands (the Moluccas, today part of Indonesia), Arab traders brought spices to and from India, whose ports welcomed ships arriving from the Spice Islands laden with pepper, ginger, nutmeg, and cinnamon.

Before refrigeration, salting was used to preserve meats and other foods. Salt was therefore extremely valuable and obtained through the Eastern trade routes. In a time when no sugar, lemons, or limes enlivened the bland dishes of Europe, spices made food palatable. Many spices were also used medicinally and compensated for pungent premodern personal hygiene. Wealthy women would wear lockets containing cloves that they would chew to freshen their breath. So valuable were spices that generous use of them in cooking was a status symbol among European nobility. One pound of ginger demanded a sheep in trade, and spices—most commonly pepper—were used as currency in place of money. As late as the reign of Queen Elizabeth I, guards on the docks of London were ordered to sew their pockets shut to prevent theft from cargoes of peppercorns.

Most important, Polo also revealed to a broad audience the secret so zealously guarded by Arab traders: the source of the spices so valued by Europe. Europeans had heard rumors of the fabled Spice Islands for centuries, but no one knew precisely where the islands lay. The location of India was well known in the late 13th century, and the Italian republics knew that opening India to trade directly with Europe would bypass the Arab monopoly and increase profits for Italian merchants. In 1291, Genoa had sent Tedisio Doria with the brothers Ugolino and Sorleone Vivaldo to find a sea route to India. All three men disappeared on the voyage, along with their crews and two galleys.

THE BEGINNING OF PORTUGUESE EXPLORATION

Challenged by the Arab control of sea routes from India and determined to end the Italian domination of imports to Europe, Portugal emerged as the first European nation to reach out from its shores successfully. The prince of Portugal, Infante Dom Henrique, who became known as Prince Henry the Navigator, initiated Portugal's overseas possessions in 1415 when he led an army to conquer the city of Ceuta, located in Morocco, opposite the key port of Gibraltar. Legend credits Henry with establishing a

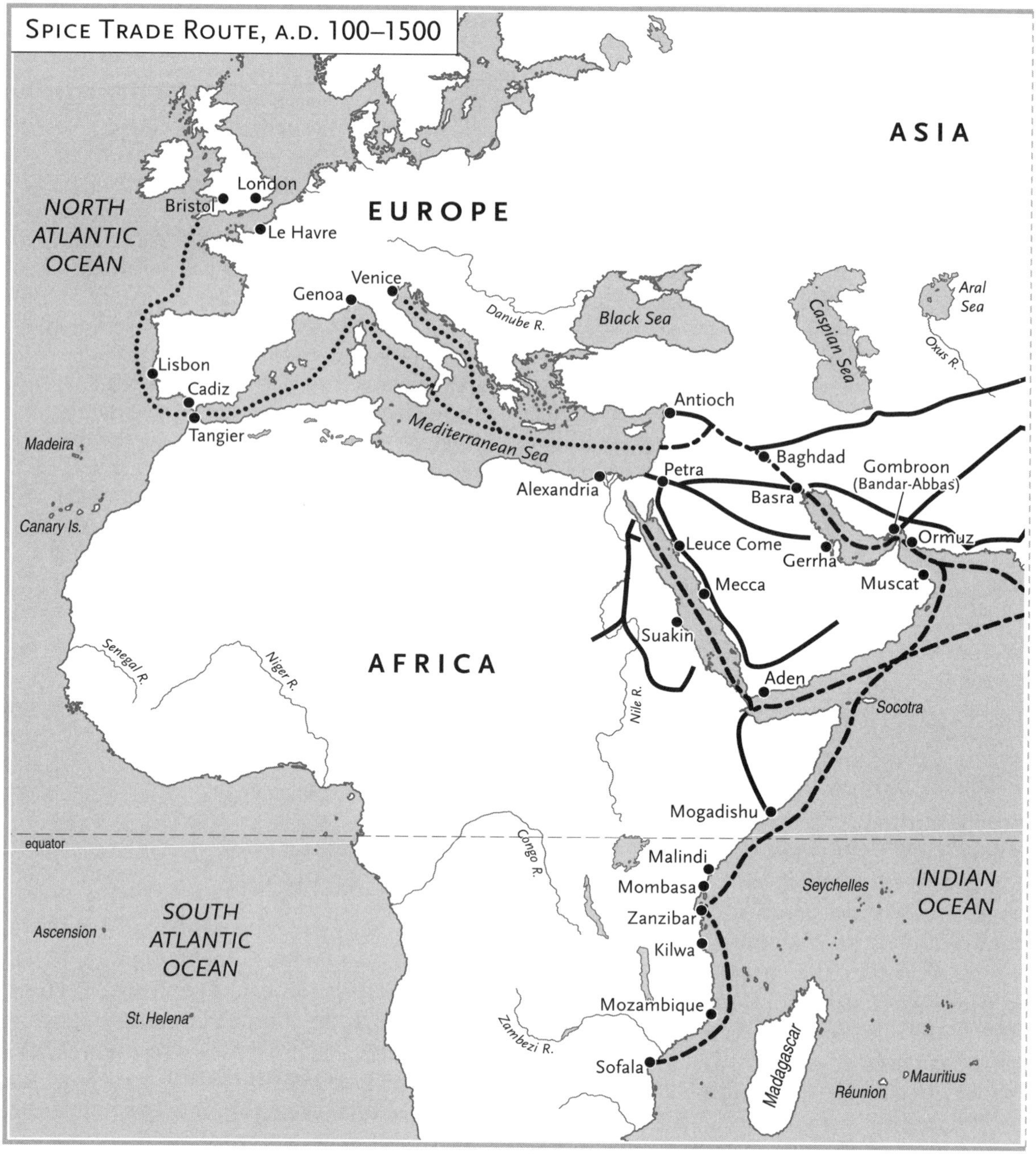

SPICE TRADE ROUTE, A.D. 100–1500

ASIA

EUROPE

London
Bristol
Le Havre

NORTH ATLANTIC OCEAN

Venice
Genoa

Danube R.   **Black Sea**

Caspian Sea   **Aral Sea**

Lisbon
Cadiz

Oxus R.

Antioch

Tangier

Baghdad

Madeira

Mediterranean Sea

Petra

Gombroon
(Bandar-Abbas)

Alexandria

Basra

Canary Is.

Leuce Come

Ormuz

Gerrha

Mecca

Muscat

AFRICA

Suakin

Senegal R.

Niger R.

Nile R.

Aden

Socotra

Mogadishu

equator

Congo R.

Malindi

Mombasa

Seychelles

INDIAN OCEAN

Zanzibar

Ascension

SOUTH ATLANTIC OCEAN

Kilwa

St. Helena

Zambezi R.

Mozambique

Sofala

Madagascar

Réunion   *Mauritius*

school of navigation on the coast of Portugal at Sagres, but modern historians consider the school to be a myth. It is clear that Henry

assembled around him a forerunner of modern research institutes, employing the best scholars of mathematics, navigation, astron-

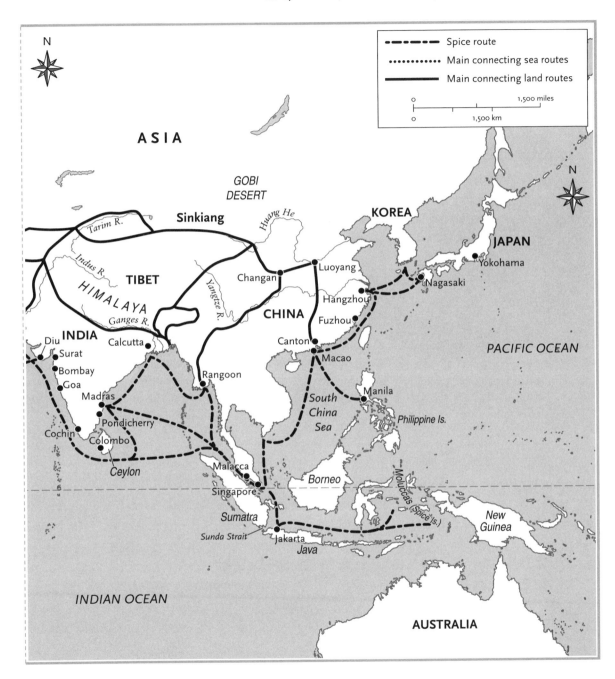

omy, and cartography as he prepared to sponsor sea expeditions. Henry's experts included Muslims skilled in astronomy and knowledgeable in the use of the Arab-developed astrolabe. His chief cartographer was a Spanish Jew named Jehuda Cresques. Prince

This astrolabe, an instrument used to determine latitude, dates from the 17th century. *(National Archives of Canada)*

Henry charged Cresques with assembling a master map, the *Padrao,* to document Portugal's discoveries and establish its claims to new territories. Henry established a shipbuilding center at Lagos, near Sagres, and there a new type of ship, the caravel, was developed. Caravels were light, maneuverable crafts fashioned after the dhows used by Arab traders. In them, Portuguese sailors would carry out a series of expeditions along the African coast and into the Atlantic Ocean.

In 1453, Europe experienced a catastrophe. The Ottoman Turks gained control of Constantinople, the most important trading exchange between the East and Europe. In capturing Constantinople the Ottoman Empire became the most powerful military, economic, and political power on Earth. Muslims controlled all access to the spice trade through the Mediterranean and northern Africa and were well positioned to invade much of Europe. The imperative for European nations to find a sea route to India and the East was greater than ever.

In 1788, Bartolomeu Dias rounded the Cape of Good Hope, a portion of which is shown in this undated photograph. *(National Archives of Canada)*

Visible in this image's background are caravels, ships used for coastal exploration during the 15th and 16th centuries. *(Library of Congress, Prints and Photographs Division [LC-USZ62-104323])*

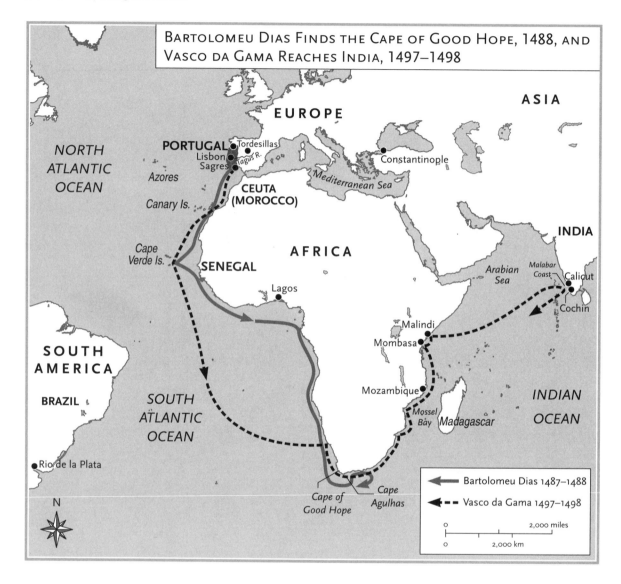

BARTOLOMEU DIAS FINDS THE CAPE OF GOOD HOPE, 1488, AND VASCO DA GAMA REACHES INDIA, 1497–1498

Enlisting in the campaign to outflank the ambitions of the Ottomans, Pope Nicholas V issued a bull, a legal pronouncement, entitled *Romanus Pontifex* on January 8, 1455. The pope granted to Portugal the right to explore and claim all of the Indies, south and east. This put Portugal in a position to gain control of the spice trade and to claim possessions in India. Capitalizing on the rights granted in *Romanus Pontifex,* Portugal interpreted the document to mean that no other nation could seek a sea route around Africa.

By the time of Henry's death in 1460, he had sponsored voyages as far into the Atlantic as the Azores, 800 miles west of Africa, and as far south on the African coast as present-day Senegal. The chief economic gain of Henry's activities, one with profound consequences for the West, was the beginning of the trade in African slaves to Europe. Henry had also established Portugal's reputation as the preeminent European power at sea. Still, attempts to find a passage around Africa to India escaped even Portugal's most daring sailors.

Portuguese King João II continued royal support for expeditions that gradually progressed farther and farther down the African coast. Medieval legend told of a Christian king named Prester John who ruled more than 72 countries in Africa that were rich in gold and silver, and João wanted to find the kingdom and establish trade. In 1487 he commanded Bartolomeu Dias to undertake a voyage to the most southern part of Africa in search of Prester John. Prester John remained a myth, but Dias's accomplishment was very real. Setting sail from the port of Tagus in midsummer, Dias commanded two caravels. A supply ship, captained by his brother Pero Dias, accompanied the caravels. The crew included six Africans who were brought to serve as translators, and the cargo included large stone pillars that were used to mark, and claim for Portugal, each important landfall made on the African coast.

In January 1488, Dias's ships were driven by storms south of the tip of Africa. By early February the expedition was 170 miles northeast of the cape at Mossel Bay. Sailing back along the south coast of Africa, Dias found the southernmost point of the continent, Cape Algulhas. It was only on the return voyage that Dias found the cape itself. Because of difficult weather he had encountered, Dias named the cape Cabo Tormentoso ("cape of storms"). The ships anchored at the cape for a month to record its features for mapmakers at home. Dias also erected a stone cross to claim the cape for his king. Upon his return to Portugal,

Dias's achievement—establishing that a sea route to the Indian Ocean existed south of the African continent—was celebrated by King João II, who renamed the new discovery Cape of Good Hope.

THE SPANISH CHALLENGE THE PORTUGUESE

Portugal's successes did not go unnoticed by other European powers. As the Spanish rulers Ferdinand and Isabella worked to consolidate Spain into one strong political unit, they also wished to gain control of the spice trade before the Portuguese did. *Romanus Pontifex* effectively prevented Spain from attempting to reach India by going around Africa. The Spanish monarchy then underwrote the 1492 expedition of Christopher Columbus that aimed to reach the Indies by sailing west. Columbus, of course, came upon the islands of the Caribbean, but he was sure they were the easternmost islands of the East, perhaps even Japan. Columbus, who carried a copy of Marco Polo's *Travels* with him on the expedition, was also certain that the voyage had taken him near the fabled continent of Locach. On his return to Spain, Columbus assured Ferdinand and Isabella that the Spice Islands would shortly belong to Spain.

The Spanish monarchs needed to protect their claim to the new route and to the Indies when Spanish ships finally reached them. In May 1493, Pope Alexander VI issued a bull, *Inter Caetera,* determining a line of demarcation that divided the Earth in two. Spain would claim the western half, and Portugal the eastern. The pope cited the spread of Christianity as the reason for his support of exploration.

We have indeed learned that you, who for a long time had intended to seek out and discover certain islands and mainlands remote and unknown and not hitherto discovered by others, to that end you might bring to the worship of our Redeemer and the profession of the Catholic faith to their residents . . .

At the time the bull was issued, Portugal had not yet actually realized the promise of

During his first voyage, Vasco da Gama sailed from Lisbon, Portugal, to Calicut, on the southwest coast of present-day India, and back by rounding the newly named Cape of Good Hope. *(Library of Congress, Prints and Photographs Division [LC-USZC4-2070])*

Dias's route by sending its ships around Africa to India. Outraged by what it considered favoritism on the part of Pope Alexander VI, who was Spanish by birth, Portugal threatened Spain with war. Realizing that war at home would be costly and would jeopardize prospects for further expeditions across the Atlantic, in 1494, Spain offered to negotiate with Portugal. Diplomats from both countries met in northwest Spain, at the town of Tordesillas. They agreed the world would be divided between Spain and Portugal, but moved the line of demarcation dividing east and west so that it lay about 370 leagues west of the Cape Verde Islands. The Capitulacion (treaty) of Tordesillas determined the course of exploration for the next century.

Four years later Portugal finally realized its ambition to reach India. Vasco da Gama, sent by the Portuguese monarchy, sailed around Africa and on May 20, 1498, reached Calicut on the Malabar Coast of southwest India. Although he lost half his fleet and had not returned with any great treasures, da Gama had won the great prize. He had opened India to Portuguese traders. Private investors supported the second Portuguese expedition to India. Because da Gama had not brought back trade goods, the crown was reluctant to finance the voyage of explorer Pedro Álvares Cabral. With 13 ships and 1,200 men, including Bartolomeu Dias, Cabral left Portugal in March 1500. Intending to follow da Gama's route around Africa, Cabral first sailed far west, into the Atlantic, and reached the eastern shore of South America. Fortunately this was territory that the Treaty of Tordesillas granted to Portugal. Cabral called the newly claimed shore Isla Vera Cruz, although its name was later changed to Brazil. Sailing east from South America, Cabral lost many ships and men as he rounded the Cape of Good Hope. Dias was among the dead. Cabral

Vasco da Gama sailed around Africa, becoming the first European to reach India by water. In this painting, da Gama stands in the prow of a rowboat being powered by his crew. *(Library of Congress, Prints and Photographs Division [LC-USZC4-2069])*

reached India—first Calicut and then Cochin. He returned to Portugal with a cargo of spices, rewarding his investors with their first profits from the spice trade.

Portugal sent Alfonso (Afonso) de Albuquerque to Cochin in 1503 to defend its trading ships against Arab raiders. In 1509, Albuquerque was made Viceroy of India and soon set out to increase Portugal's reach in the Indies. He first sent Diego López de Sequeira to Malacca, on the Malay Peninsula, to survey possibilities there. Albuquerque then overthrew the Muslim rulers of Goa, in southern India, in 1510. Goa at once became the staging ground for Portuguese expeditions, which established armed trading posts as they ventured closer to the Spice Islands themselves. In 1511, 1,400 men captured Malacca, and Portugal's monopoly on the spice routes was ensured. Albuquerque sent his ships to the Spice Islands in 1512, and within a year Portuguese bases on Ternate and Batjan were sending spice-filled cargo ships back to Lisbon. The riches of the East were Portugal's, and its king was aptly called Manuel the Fortunate. Manuel designed a new title for himself, one that reflects the power and ambition of his nation: Lord of the Conquest, Navigation, and Commerce of India, Ethiopia, Arabia, and Persia.

SPAIN GAINS THE NEW WORLD

While Portugal grew rich from its possessions in India and the Spice Islands, Spanish expeditions sought fortune across the Atlantic. While it became clear that Columbus had not found the East, or even a western route to the Indies, Spain realized that the New World might itself prove to be lucrative and sent its men and ships to explore the Caribbean and the lands to its north and south. Florentine sailor Amerigo Vespucci undertook the most notable

exploration and promotion of the New World in the early 16th century. Vespucci was employed by the Spanish Crown and named its chief navigator in 1508. So enthusiastic was his publicizing of Spain's new possessions that mapmakers began to label the southern part of these lands "Amerige," or America.

America, within the goal of finding a western route to the Indies, in many ways seemed an obstacle to be gotten around—or gotten across. The Spanish soldier Vasco Núñez de

Francisco Pizarro's connection to exploration began when he joined Hernán Cortés, a relative, on a journey to Hispaniola, where he would later accept an opportunity to work with Vasco Núñez de Balboa. *(Library of Congress, Prints and Photographs Division [LC-USZ62-104354])*

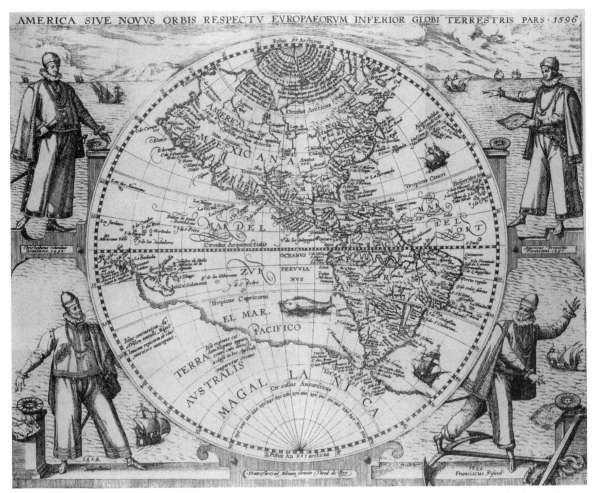

AMERICA SIVE NOVVS ORBIS RESPECTV EVROPAEORVM INFERIOR GLOBI TERRESTRIS PARS · 1596

An engraving by Theodore de Bry, this late 15th-century map of the Americas is bordered by (clockwise from top left) Christopher Columbus, Amerigo Vespucci, Ferdinand Magellan, and Francisco Pizarro. *(Library of Congress, Prints and Photographs Division [LC-USZ62-89908])*

Balboa heard stories about a land where, he wrote, "men ride camels and even the cooking pots are made of gold." A great ocean washed the shores of this land. Balboa, an ambitious self-promoter, had taken part in Spanish enterprises in the New World for about a decade. In 1513 he was the acting governor of the Spanish colony at Darién, on the Isthmus of Panama, and married to a Panamanian Indian named Caretita. Indians had told him that the treasure-filled land was just over the mountains of Darién. Balboa, a party of 190 men that included Francisco Pizarro (who went on to conquer Peru), and several hundred Indian allies set out to find the rumored sea. Advancing about one mile a day, the expedition battled three weeks over mountains, through rain forests, across swollen and flooding rivers, and into swamps. Many men contracted malaria. Others died in conflicts with unfriendly Indians, although the mortality rate for the native people was higher. One report tells of the Spanish killing 600 Indians in one day of the journey.

On September 26, 1513, Balboa and his men came out of the jungle and climbed up one last mountain. On its summit, Balboa, as the 19th-century English poet John Keats wrote, "stared at the Pacific—and all his men looked at each other with a wild surmise— silent, upon a peak in Darien." Balboa named the seemingly endless waters Mar del Sur (the South Sea) because he had reached it by trav-

Balboa first spotted the Pacific Ocean, as shown in this undated drawing, after crossing the Isthmus of Panama in 1513. *(National Archives of Canada)*

Vasco Núñez de Balboa governed the Spanish colony at Darién. *(Library of Congress)*

eling south across the isthmus. The expedition marched three more days and reached the shore on September 29. Balboa, still in his armor and carrying an icon of the Virgin Mary and Jesus in one hand and the banner of the royal house of Spain in the other, ceremoniously walked into the water. His men were overjoyed to find that the water tasted of salt because that confirmed they had found a great ocean, not an inland lake. According to Peter Martyr, an historian who wrote during the time of the exploration, Balboa claimed for Spain "these seas and lands and islands and all the lands thereunto annexed until the final day of judgment."

In this illustration published in 1859, Balboa claims the Pacific Ocean for Spain.
(National Archives of Canada)

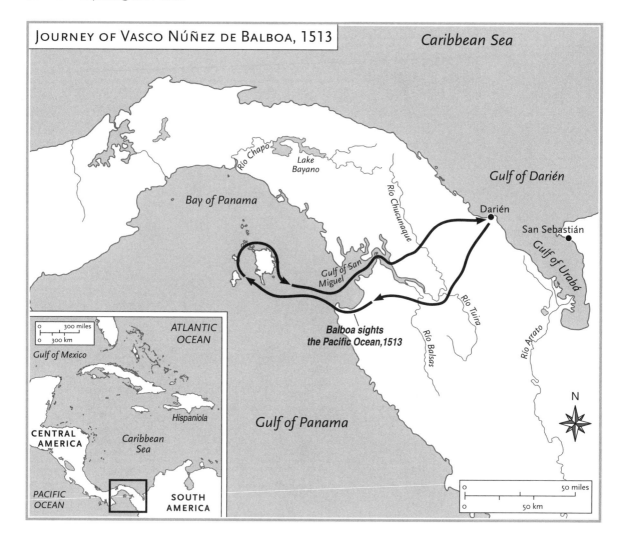

JOURNEY OF VASCO NÚÑEZ DE BALBOA, 1513

Caribbean Sea

Rio Chapo
Lake Bayano
Gulf of Darién
Bay of Panama
Rio Chucunaque
Darién
San Sebastián
Gulf of San Miguel
Gulf of Urabá
Balboa sights the Pacific Ocean, 1513
Rio Tuira
Rio Balsas
Rio Arrato

0   300 miles
0   300 km
ATLANTIC OCEAN
Gulf of Mexico
Hispaniola
CENTRAL AMERICA
Caribbean Sea
Gulf of Panama
PACIFIC OCEAN
SOUTH AMERICA

N

0   50 miles
0   50 km

News of Balboa's great discovery, along with quantities of gold that the expedition had found in Panama, reached Spain within months. Balboa himself was not so lucky. Political rivals who wanted the profits from Balboa's gold discoveries accused him of treason, and Balboa was beheaded in Panama in 1519. King Ferdinand, an aged man at 64, became determined to pursue a western route to the Indies even more vigorously. Portugal's

hold on the Spice Islands was not yet firm, and the Treaty of Tordesillas allowed Spain a western trading route. Beyond the riches that even part interest in the spice trade might bring, Spain entertained dreams of finding and claiming Marco Polo's Locach, the land covered with gold, Terra Australis Incognita, the Great Southern Continent.

A sea passage around South America was as eagerly sought by the Spanish as the passage around Africa had been by the Portuguese. In 1515, Juan Díaz de Solís, the chief pilot of Spain who had made the first charts of the South American coast in 1506, led a flotilla of three ships to search for a passage. Solís sailed as far south as 40° latitude and explored the mouth of the Rio de la Plata, in present-day Argentina, thinking that the wide river might be the western passage. Solís and several crewmembers were cannibalized by Indians during a landing on the banks of the Río de la Plata. His crew watched from the ships in horror, immediately abandoned exploration of the river, and returned to Spain without finding the passage.

The Spanish were convinced that a strait, a passage to the newly found ocean, had to exist in the New World's southern hemisphere. Geographers and cartographers shared this conviction. Globes constructed by the German geographer Johannes Schöner in 1515 and 1520 indicated that such a strait might exist between the Atlantic and Pacific Oceans. Such bold conjecture would prove to be right.

4

MAGELLAN'S CIRCUMNAVIGATION, 1519–1522

Fernão de Magalhães, although born in the landlocked Tráz-o-Montez region, seemed destined to take part in Portugal's seaborne empire. At the age of 10, Magalhães was sent to learn the ways of the nobility at the palace of King Manuel I. The boy learned courtly manners, literature, music, and mathematics. He also received instruction in astronomy, the science of navigation, and the methods of war. At 15, Magalhães became an officer in the army of Portugal. Following Vasco da Gama's great opening of India, Portugal moved to consolidate its power over India and the Indian Ocean. In 1505, Francisco de Almeida was sent as viceroy of India. Magalhães and his cousin Francisco Serrão went with Almeida's fleet. For the next seven years Magalhães participated in Portuguese campaigns to control India and the eastern coast of Africa. In 1511 he joined the forces of Alfonso de Albuquerque in the conquest of Malacca, the port on the Malay Peninsula through which all spices headed for Europe must pass.

The next year, Magalhães returned to Lisbon, but his cousin Serrão was sent by Albuquerque to the Spice Islands to initiate Portuguese rule over the ultimate source of the precious spices. Serrão settled on the island of Ternate, married a local woman, and began to send letters describing the Spice Islands to his cousin in Portugal. His letters, and possibly charts of the Moluccas, excited his cousin's imagination and ambition. Although Magalhães returned to Portugal in glory from his ventures in the East, he had lost his share of captured treasures in two separate shipwrecks. His only property was Enrique, a Malayan slave he had bought in Malacca. Magalhães had been wounded in a 1513 campaign in Morocco, and his name had been tarnished by accusations of illegal trading.

In 1515, Magalhães drew up a plan for reaching the Spice Islands from the west. He had heard about the recent discovery of the Pacific Ocean via the Americas by Vasco Núñez de Balboa and concluded from Serrão's letters that the Spice Islands were within a few days' sail of South America. Magalhães knew that Spain had sent Juan Díaz de Solís to find a southern passage that year. If Portugal could find the strait before Spain, it would gain advantage in the race to possess the Spice Islands. Despite all these compelling reasons, when Magalhães presented a proposal for an expedition to King Manuel, he was denied. The king had no reason to entrust a soldier with a tainted reputation with such a voyage, and furthermore he could not afford the project. Portugal had concentrated its money, men, and ships in the Indian Ocean.

FROM PORTUGAL TO SPAIN

King Manuel I's insult infuriated and humiliated Magalhães. He withdrew from Lisbon to coastal Oporto. There he studied maps and logs of previous expeditions to South America and became convinced a passage to the South Sea must exist in southern America. He decided to take his proposal to the Spanish court. In October 1517, Magalhães renounced his loyalty to Portugal and went to Seville, Spain's most important maritime center. He took a Spanish name, Hernando de Magallanes, translated in the English-speaking world as "Ferdinand Magellan." Spain had a new king in 1518, 17-year-old Charles I, whose rule extended beyond Spain and its possessions in the New World to the Netherlands and parts of Italy. Charles was the heir to the Holy Roman Empire, a union led by Austria created in A.D. 962 to ally the principalities and small nations of western Europe. Charles knew he would soon be the ruler of all of Europe (except Portugal, France, and England), however limited military and financial resources jeopardized his current position. Unlike Manuel, Charles was willing to wager his meager fortunes at the prospect of immense profits. Charles granted funds for the expedition

on March 22, 1518. An agreement was drawn up to divide the expected profits and to designate Magellan as the governor of any newly discovered territories. The king ordered the Spanish agency controlling trade, the Casa de Contratacíon, to outfit an armada for the expedition. Five ships—the *Trinidad*, the *San Antonio*, the *Concepción*, the *Victoria*, and the *Santiago*—were purchased and refitted. Sebastián Álvarez, a Portuguese diplomat in Seville, doubted that the ships would withstand the voyage. He wrote to the Portuguese court, "I would not care to sail to the Canaries in such crates. Their ribs are as soft as butter."

Charles appointed Magellan commander of the armada. This antagonized its Spanish captains, who hated that a Spanish expedition

Spain financed the journey in which Ferdinand Magellan and his crew attempted to circumnavigate the globe. *(Library of Congress, Prints and Photographs Division [LC-USZ62-92885])*

would make a very wealthy man of the Portuguese turncoat. The armada, dubbed the Armada of the Moluccas, had a crew of 237 men of many nations. Most were Spanish, but sailors from Portugal, Ireland, England, and the Netherlands signed on. Magellan's Malayan slave, Enrique, accompanied him to serve as translator, and African slaves may well have sailed with the armada. Italian sailor Antonio Pigafetta kept a journal during his adventure that remains the best record of the voyage. Pigafetta wrote that he "was desirous of sailing so that I might see the wonders of the world." The ships' holds were filled with provisions for a long journey, as well as with 10,000 fish hooks, 20,000 bells, mirrors, combs, knives, and bracelets to barter for food with native peoples along the route.

The men of the Armada of the Moluccas attended a mass in Seville to consecrate the expedition. During the ceremony Magellan swore allegiance to Charles, now Holy Roman Emperor, and received a royal flag from him. Monks of Seville were given funds to pray for the success of the enterprise. Magellan steeled himself for the unknown by writing a last letter to his wife and by preparing a will. The will directed how his shares of the profits from the expedition should be directed and ordered that his slave, Enrique, should be freed. Magellan, his officers, and the crew boarded the ships and proceeded from Seville down the Guadalquivir River to the coast. The fleet sailed from Sanlúcar de Barrameda on September 20, 1519.

FROM SPAIN TO PATAGONIA

Almost from the day of its departure, the expedition encountered difficulties. The course set by most Spanish ships heading to the Americas was to sail into the Atlantic from the Canary Islands. Located off the northwest coast of Africa, the islands had long served as a station for final provisioning. Magellan's ships did pause in the Canaries, but then Magellan announced that he intended to sail down the coast of Africa almost to the equator and then set out into the ocean. The captain of the *San Antonio,* Juan de Cartegena, had led the opposition to Magellan during the preparations for the voyage. He now argued to the other captains that Magellan was leading them into a trap, that Portuguese warships awaited them in the waters off Africa. Magellan responded to Cartegena's challenge by relieving him of command of the *San Antonio* and throwing him in chains.

The armada's unconventional route allowed it to evade Portuguese ships, but in sail-

ing so close to the equator, the fleet fell victim to other enemies. The Atlantic pitched the ships into squalls worse than even the most experienced sailor had ever seen. To prevent the ships from being blown over, their sails were struck. The ships were then at the winds' mercy, and captains had little control over the ships' course. In the middle of the ocean Magellan's ships became caught in the doldrums, a zone of breathless wind. For weeks the men endured beating sun and unbearable thirst. Salted meat taken onboard in the Canary Islands began to rot and stink until it had to be thrown overboard.

Finally, on December 13, Magellan's ships entered the harbor of Rio de Janeiro. Although Brazil was claimed by Portugal under the Treaty of Tordesillas, no colony had yet been established, and the Spanish fleet was free to spend two weeks there, recovering from the Atlantic crossing and trading with the area's indigenous people, bartering fish hooks and bells for fresh food and game. Magellan knew that the Southern Hemisphere's summer was coming to a close. He wanted to find the passage to the South Sea, or at least get as far south as he could before the weather grew cold and the seas rough.

Leaving Rio on December 26, the armada followed the South American coast as they explored inlets and rivers, hoping to find the strait. Spying a high peak, Magellan is said to have exclaimed, "I see a mountain!" and thus gave a name to the city that was later established there, Montevideo (present-day Uruguay). Just south of this mountain a great bay

This map, published in the early 1600s, portrays ships sailing through the Strait of Magellan's circuitous path. On the bottom right, some Patagonians greet Dutch explorers. *(Library of Congress, Prints and Photographs Division [LC-USZ62-71980])*

opened to the sea. The crew became excited; perhaps they had found the strait already. Magellan realized, because its water was fresh and unchanged by tides, that they had found the mouth of the river where Solís, searching for the strait, had been killed four years before. Magellan named the river in honor of Solís, although it is now known as Rio de la Plata.

By late March 1520, winter was approaching. The men began to see penguins and seals along the coast. They called the seals "sea wolves" and the penguins *patos sin alas* ("ducks without wings"). They saw Indians on shore so tall the Spanish called them *patos gones* ("Big Feet"). But they had not found the strait, and many were beginning to believe that they never would. At 49° 15' south latitude the ships reached a protected harbor Magellan named Puerto San Julián. The captains of the other four ships came to Magellan on the *Trinidad.* They told him all the crew wanted to go back to Spain. The region, called Patagonia after its big-footed inhabitants, was too barren to sustain them through the winter. Winds, ice, and snow endangered the ships. Magellan refused their request and ordered the crews to prepare for wintering at San Julián.

The night before Easter, mutiny broke out. Antonio Pigafetta recorded the event in his journal. "In this port three of the ships rose up against the Captain-major, their captains saying that they intended to take him to Castle in arrest, as he was taking them all to destruction." The captain of the *Victoria,* Luis de Mendoza, freed Cartagena, who then took command of the *San Antonio.* Gaspar de Quesada, captain of the *Concepción,* joined the two. When the sun rose, three of Magellan's five ships and 170 members of his crew were in rebellion. The mutineers sent a boat to the *Trinidad* with a message: They would spare

Magellan his life if he agreed to take the expedition back to Spain. In reply, Magellan sent his most loyal officer, Gonzalo Gómez de Espinosa, to the *Victoria* to force surrender. When Mendoza refused the terms with a sneer, Espinosa slit his throat. Espinosa signaled to loyalists on the other ships, and a battle for control of the expedition began. Espinosa strung up Mendoza's body on the rigging, warning rebels of their fate if they failed to surrender. Magellan blockaded the port with his loyal ships. By midnight, both Cartagena and Quesada had surrendered.

After reassuring himself that he was again in command of the expedition, Magellan ordered his crew to take the body of Luis de Mendoza ashore, where it was drawn and quartered. The pieces of the corpse were impaled on poles and displayed for all the crew to see. Quesada's servant was directed to cut off his master's head. Cartegena and a priest who had aided the mutiny were left behind when the ships sailed. Forty other men were sentenced to death, with the sentence commuted to hard labor while the ship remained at Puerto San Julián.

Labor at Puerto San Julián was hard for the entire crew. Shelters had to be built to house everyone through the winter. Sailors repaired the hulls of the ships after careening them, dragging the ships ashore and turning them on their sides. Others hunted, fished, and trapped. An inventory revealed that dealers in Seville had swindled Magellan. Since supplies of biscuits and salted beef would certainly be rationed once the expedition reached the South Sea, extra stores of salted meat and fish needed to be prepared. Magellan decided to send the *Santiago* on one last search for the strait before the coldest weather set in. He thought proof of the strait's existence would improve morale and enable the crew to endure a hard winter in port. The *Santiago* did

Mutiny

Ferdinand Magellan's treatment of Luis de Mendoza, Gaspar de Quesada, and the other mutineers may seem inhumanly cruel, but mutiny was considered the worst violation of military law. Captains were themselves judged by the order kept on their ship, and sailors who broke rules were punished immediately and publicly. The sight of a shipmate flogged with a cat o' nine tails until he was drenched in his own blood was intended to serve as a warning. A thief on board could be made to run the gauntlet, to walk between two lines of his mates as each sailor whipped him. Despite a system of strict order and severe penalties, commanders of early oceanic voyages constantly feared mutiny. Even the great Italian explorer Christopher Columbus sailed with the threat of his crew mutinying over scant food and dwindling water supplies.

Brutal conditions were common on sailing voyages well into the 19th century, and sailors were often driven to starvation and exhaustion. Mutiny sometimes seemed like a reasonable choice between almost certain death at sea and possible death if the mutiny failed. By the 18th century European navy ships carried soldiers called marines, whose quarters were located between those of the crew and the cabins of the officers and whose job included keeping or restoring order onboard.

The most famous mutiny in the Pacific occurred in 1789 and has become inspiration for hundreds of books and several films. The British navy sent Lieutenant William Bligh to Tahiti in 1787. The purpose of the voyage was to collect breadfruit trees, which would then be taken to the English colonies in the Caribbean and transplanted to provide food for slaves working on plantations. Sailors and officers came to see Bligh as an undisciplined leader, criticizing him for allowing the *Bounty* to deteriorate to the point of its sails rotting during its five-month stay in Tahiti. On April 28, 1789, three weeks after leaving Tahiti to carry the trees to the Caribbean, the crew rose up against Bligh. Led by junior officer Fletcher Christian, the mutiny was bloodless. Bligh and men loyal to him were set adrift in a 23-foot boat. Remarkably, Bligh led his supporters across 3,618 miles of ocean, surviving to reach the island of Timor on June 14.

The *Bounty* returned to Tahiti. Most of the crew chose to stay in what they had come to regard as a tropical paradise. But Christian assembled colonists—nine *Bounty* crewmembers, six Tahitian men, and 12 Tahitian women—and set sail on September 22, 1789. In the course of searching for an isolated, habitable island, the *Bounty* became the first European ship to find the island of Rarotonga. Coming at last to Pitcairn Island, a mountainous island surrounded by treacherous surf, Christian landed his followers and brought ashore animals, plants, supplies, and anything usable from the *Bounty*. The *Bounty* was then sunk. Descendants of the *Bounty* mutineers still live on Pitcairn Island.

find a great, salty river 60 miles south of Puerto San Julián but was then wrecked during a storm. Two survivors walked 11 miles through ice and snow to summon a rescue party for the remaining 37 crewmen. The loss of the *Santiago* only worsened the mood of the expedition.

In August, still winter, Magellan's ships left Puerto San Julián to continue their voyage southward. At 50° south latitude, near the Falkland Islands, the crew rose up against Magellan once again. It was October and no strait had been found. Many felt it did not exist. Many of the crew also felt that the best thing to do would be to sail east to the Cape of Good Hope. Then they could either sail into the Indian Ocean and on to the Moluccas or return to Spain. Magellan made a bargain. If no strait were found in the next weeks, he would agree to sail east. On October 21 the fleet rounded a headland Magellan named the Cape of 11,000 Virgins. The *San Antonio* and the *Concepción* were ordered to sail into the broad inlet to the south of this cape. Immediately the ships were sucked into the pounding surf just as a horrendous storm arose. As he lost sight of his ships, Magellan was sure he had sent many men to their death. For two days the storm raged around the *Trinidad* and the *Victoria*, breaking the *Victoria*'s mast. As the sea calmed, Magellan prepared to head back to Spain, unwilling to continue with only two ships. Then, miraculously, the sails of the *San Antonio* and the *Concepción* appeared on the horizon.

THROUGH THE STRAIT AND INTO THE SOUTH SEA

The lost ships were greeted with music, cannon fire, and singing. Their captains reported that they had come to a point in the passage where the ebb tides and flood tides were equally strong and the water was salty. They had found the strait. In honor of the saints who had protected the expedition, Magellan named

The Strait of Magellan appears vast and is lined by snow-covered mountains, visible in the distance of this century-old photograph. *(Library of Congress, Prints and Photographs Division [LC-USZ62-119654])*

This early 17th-century map includes the Strait of Magellan, as well as the imagined topography of the surrounding land. *(Library of Congress, Prints and Photographs Division [LC-USZ62-71977])*

the strait Canal de Todos Santos. It bears his name today. The ships entered the strait, and powerful currents drove the ships close to rocky, towering cliffs and threatened to ground them on the many craggy islands. At night, watchmen could see the fires of Indian settlements, and this lead them to call the region Tierra del Fuego (Land of Fire). Midway through the passage, the crew of the *San Antonio* became convinced that Magellan had made another mistake and turned around. The *San Antonio* sailed back to Spain, taking with it more than a third of the armada's provisions.

After 38 days and 373 miles of hard sailing, Magellan saw a headland and, beyond it, open ocean. He named the headland Cap Deseado (Cape Desire) because he had longed to reach it. It was November 28, 1520. Pigafetta wrote in his journal, "We debouched from that strait, engulfing ourselves in the Pacific Sea." Entering the calm at the end of the strait, Magellan was so grateful he fell to his knees crying. He called the ocean Mar Pacífica ("peaceful sea") because it was so blessedly peaceful. A priest accompanying the expedition recited the blessing of Our Lady of Victory and hymns were sung. Magellan's men rejoiced because they thought the object of their expedition, the Spice Islands, were only days away. Their spirits were lightened by the warm trade winds that guided the ships in to the Pacific. "Well was it named Pacific, for during this period we met with no storms," recorded Pigafetta.

With no maps, because no Europeans had ever sailed these waters, the ships meandered west without sighting a single island. Pilot Francisco Albo recorded the armada's route and his notes make it clear that slight variations in their course would have lead the ships to the Marquesas or to Tahiti. A month out from the strait, men began to die of hunger and disease. The penguins, fish, and seals that had been salted at Puerto San Julián were rot-

ting. Maggots infested the ships, even eating the sailors' clothing. Many men were severely weakened by scurvy, a potentially fatal defi-

Magellan's ships, imagined in this drawing, sailed safely through the strait discovered near the southern tip of South America. *(National Archives of Canada)*

ciency of vitamin C. By early February the ships had found two islands—Puka Puka in the Tuamotu group and nearby Flint Island—but they were so barren that Magellan called them Las Desaventuradas (the Unfortunate Islands).

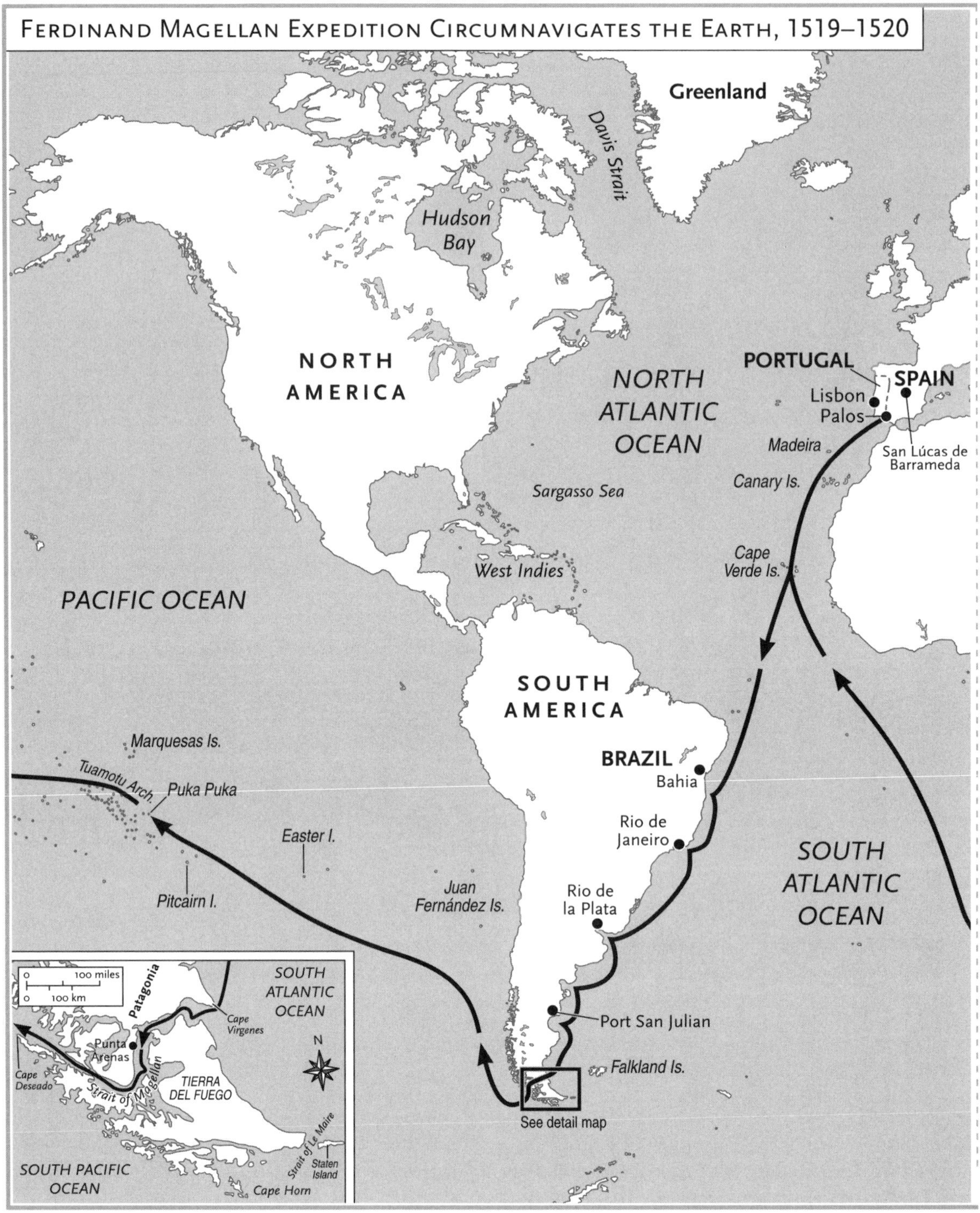
FERDINAND MAGELLAN EXPEDITION CIRCUMNAVIGATES THE EARTH, 1519–1520
Greenland
Davis Strait
Hudson Bay
NORTH AMERICA
NORTH ATLANTIC OCEAN
PORTUGAL
SPAIN
Lisbon
Palos
San Lúcas de Barrameda
Madeira
Canary Is.
Sargasso Sea
Cape Verde Is.
West Indies
PACIFIC OCEAN
SOUTH AMERICA
BRAZIL
Bahia
Rio de Janeiro
Rio de la Plata
Marquesas Is.
Tuamotu Arch.
Puka Puka
Easter I.
Pitcairn I.
Juan Fernández Is.
SOUTH ATLANTIC OCEAN
Port San Julian
Falkland Is.
See detail map
100 miles
100 km
Patagonia
SOUTH ATLANTIC OCEAN
Cape Virgenes
Punta Arenas
Cape Deseado
Strait of Magellan
TIERRA DEL FUEGO
N
Strait of Le Maire
Staten Island
SOUTH PACIFIC OCEAN
Cape Horn

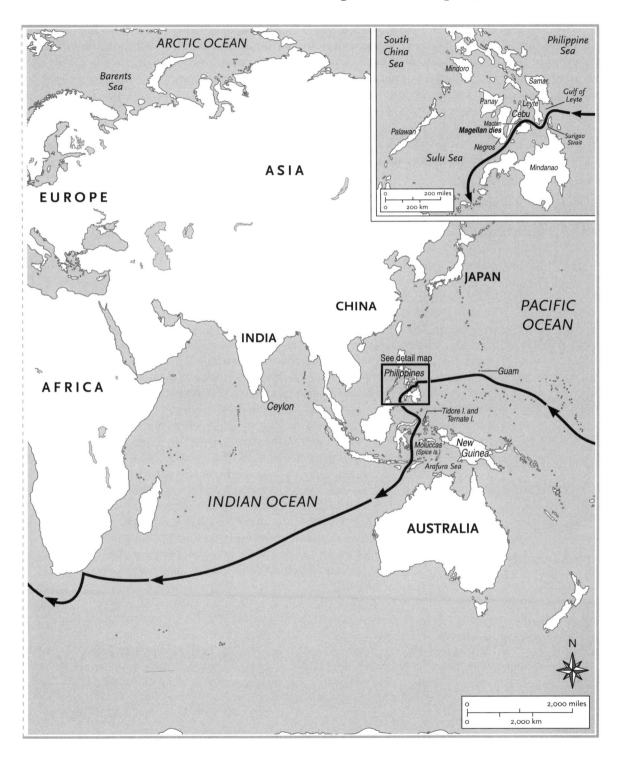

The ships crossed the equator on February 13. Food rations had been cut to the point that one sailor wrote, "We only ate old biscuit reduced to powder and stinking with the dirt rats had made on it." Men paid half a ducat for a rat. By March even rats were gone on the ships, and the *Trinidad* was completely out of food. Its crew was removing the ox hides that protected the masts from friction caused by ropes and eating it. Men made cakes by

Circumnavigators and Privateers

Fifty-five years would pass between Magellan's great feat of circumnavigation and the next successful sailing voyage around the world. Before 1600 only five expeditions were successful in circumnavigating the globe. The shortest route from Europe and back was from west to east, passing through the Strait of Magellan with its fierce winds behind a ship's sails. Most early circumnavigators, however, went in the opposite direction and sailed around Africa's Cape of Good Hope, counting on better weather and established ports. Indeed, the motive for circumnavigation was not strong for the European powers in the 16th century. Trade routes to the Spice Islands were well established. Spanish ships going from South America to the Philippines created a global trade network readily accessed without undertaking the danger and expense of a round-the-world expedition. Thirst for exploration, a desire to challenge Spanish claims to the Pacific, and a degree of chance fueled the early circumnavigators.

All three elements certainly motivated the second circumnavigator, English privateer Francis Drake, who sailed the *Golden Hind* around the world on a privateering voyage from 1577 to 1580. Another Englishman, Thomas Cavendish, circumnavigated the globe in 1588, all the while plundering Spanish ships bearing treasure between the Philippines and Mexico. During the reign of Queen Elizabeth I, privateers were often employed by the Crown to harass the ships of England's enemies. These legally authorized pirates carried letters of marque and reprisal that protected them from prosecution for crimes at sea. The Admiralty, the basic administrative arm of the modern English Royal Navy, was established principally to regulate privateering. Authorization of privateers was an inexpensive and risk-free way for nations to pursue war. Since privateers owed 10 percent of any prize captured from enemy ships, they were a good source of income for the Crown as well.

Opposite page: Ferdinand Magellan and Francis Drake, circumnavigators of the world, are included on this title page (on the left side) from an early book about exploration. Magellan's *Victoria,* the only ship to survive of the five that began his attempt, is featured on the page. *(Library of Congress, Prints and Photographs Division [LC-USZ62-84951])* pounding maggots into meal, mixing it with sawdust and soaking it in urine.

On March 4, 1521, a lookout named Navarro sighted land. Magellan's men knelt to thank God for salvation. The ships had to sail another two days to reach the island, which was probably Guam, in the Marianas. As the ships neared the islands, men in dugout canoes paddled out to meet them. Initially the relationship between the people of the island

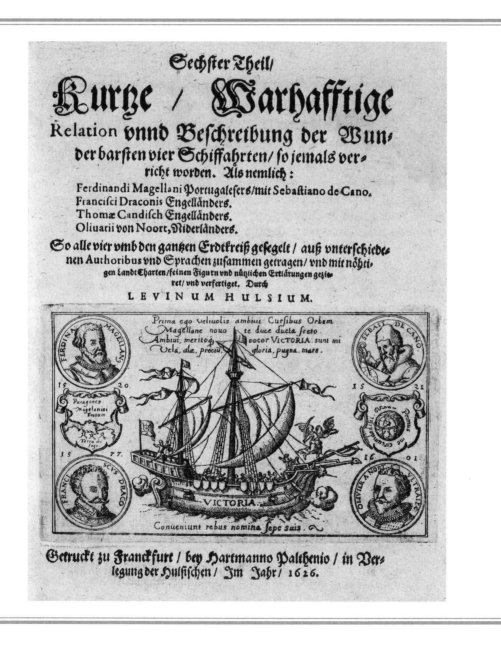

and the Spanish was friendly. Islanders brought food and water to the starved and weakened sailors. Curious about the strange boats used by the ships to ferry men and goods to the beach, islanders took the *Trinidad*'s skiff without permission. Magellan was enraged and ordered a gunner to fire a broadside into a group of houses near the shore. The islanders fled into the interior and did not return. This unfortunate pattern of misunderstanding and Spanish retribution was to become all too common. Magellan decided to leave what he had named Las Islas de Ladrones (Thieves Islands) and head to the Spice Islands.

In fact, Magellan's ships were still 1,700 miles away from the Moluccas. Magellan's course may have been determined by his desire to reach some islands located north of the Moluccas as yet unseen by Europeans but rumored to be rich in gold and silver. His agreement with King Charles meant that Magellan was to receive future profits from two of the islands discovered during the expedition. If the Islands of Lazarus, where he had brought his ships to on March 16, were the islands of rumor, Magellan would be rich beyond his dreams.

Later renamed the Philippines, the Islands of Lazarus would indeed prove to make Spanish fortunes. Sailing into a broad bay now known as the Gulf of Leyte, the armada entered the Surigao Strait. Magellan's slave, Enrique, was now able to communicate with the people of the islands. Some historians speculate that Enrique was originally from that area, not from Malaya, and when the expedition reached the Philippines, Enrique became history's first circumnavigator.

On March 28 the ships anchored off the lush island of Cebu. With Spain's desire for the gold and luxury goods of the East, there was an almost equally strong desire to bring the peoples of the new lands to salvation by converting them to Christianity. Priests had come on the expedition for this purpose. Magellan hoped that the people of Cebu would quickly abandon what he saw as their savage beliefs and embrace the Catholic faith. His hopes were rewarded when the ruler of the island, Rajah Humabon, was baptized. Through the first half of April many Cebuanos converted, including most of their leaders. On the nearby island of Mactan, people were not so easily convinced that they should give up their traditions. Their leader, Lapu Lapu, let it be known that he cared nothing for the Spanish, their priests, or their guns.

Magellan knew how to deal with insurrection. On April 27, he and 48 armed men made the brief boat trip to Mactan. Wearing heavy armor, Magellan and his men waded over the swampy shore, only to be met by more than a thousand of Lapu Lapu's people. Magellan was slain within minutes. Pigafetta mourned the loss of his commander, "They killed our mirror, our light, our comfort and our true guide."

THE ARMADA OF THE MOLUCCAS AFTER MAGELLAN

With the death of Magellan, the armada also lost its discipline. When the survivors returned to Cebu their wounds proved to the Cebuanos that the Spanish were weak, that their God gave them no special protection. No longer welcome, the men decided it was time to make the final push to the Moluccas. The remaining officers selected Juan Carvalho to be the new captain-general of the expedition. Carvalho knew that three ships could not be handled by the 115 surviving crewmembers and ordered the *Concepción* to be burned and scuttled, sunk off Cebu. He also burned Magellan's logs and papers in a final act of resentment. With Carvalho commanding the *Trinidad* and Juan de Elcano as captain of the *Victoria,* the ships sailed south, pillaging native settlements for food as they went. On November 8, the armada at last reached the Spice Islands, landing at Tidore.

The people of Tidore welcomed the ships. The Portuguese had been ruthless conquerors, and the arrival of the Spanish, with their assurances that more Spanish ships would follow, promised the downfall of Portugal's power in the Moluccas. The *Trinidad* was in terrible shape, and the ships stayed at Tidore as it was repaired. On December 21, 1521, the *Victoria,* commanded by Elcano and with a full cargo of cloves, left Tidore for Spain. The *Trinidad* sailed later and was blown off course, perhaps as far as Japan. Limping back to Tidore, the *Trinidad* was intercepted by the Portuguese. Its cargo was seized, and its crew of 53 men imprisoned. Only four of the *Trinidad*'s men made it back to Spain alive.

The *Victoria* struggled across the Indian Ocean, evading Portuguese warships all the way. Rounding the Cape of Good Hope and resting in the Cape Verde Islands, the *Victoria* arrived at Sanlúcar de Barrameda on September 6, 1522. Eighteen men remained, the first Europeans to have circumnavigated the globe. The shipment of cloves was sold for 10,000 times the price paid for them and twice what the expedition had cost. Emperor Charles V was happy with the accomplishments of the expedition. Charles had made a modest return on his investment. A route to the Spice Islands had been found to the west. The Isles of Lazarus stood fair to be conquered by future expeditions. Most important, Portugal's monopoly in the Spice Islands had been broken.

5

CONQUISTA ESPIRITUAL
The Spanish in the Pacific

 The great challenge facing Emperor Charles V, king of Spain (as Charles I) and Holy Roman Emperor, was to capitalize on the accomplishments of the Armada of the Moluccas. Even as the *Victoria* returned to Spain, Spain's rivals were moving into the Pacific. Portuguese captain Cristavao Mendonça became the first European to make a report of a great landmass south of the Spice Islands in 1522 that could be the fabled Terra Australis Incognita. France was planning to send Florentine navigator Giovanni Verrazano to discover a route to the Pacific across North America through an imagined Northwest Passage. And Spain stood on the verge of economic catastrophe. Charles had acquired huge debts in gaining the crown of the Holy Roman Empire. Only by asserting Spain's sovereignty in the Moluccas and expanding lucrative possessions in the Pacific could Charles prevent disaster.

Charles pressed Portugal to revisit the Treaty of Tordesillas and to recognize Spanish claims on the Moluccas. Since the geographic position of the islands was still unclear to

negotiators, nothing was resolved, and Spain and Portugal continued to struggle for control of the Spice Islands. Charles realized that exploration and conquest of new territories required careful administration. He authorized the Casa de Contratación to oversee all expeditions, to regulate trade, and to catalog all records, maps, and charts generated by Spanish explorers. He created the Council of the Indies to govern Spain's overseas possessions. Along with how to wrest control of the Moluccas, two puzzles occupied Charles's time in the 1520s. The first was whether Magellan's Tierra del Fuego was actually the northern tip of Terra Australis Incognita. The second was how Spain could best extract wealth from the Islands of Lazarus.

SPAIN'S GUERILLA WAR IN THE SPICE ISLANDS

In 1525 Emperor Charles V sent soldier Francisco García Jofre de Loaysa and the hero of the *Victoria,* Juan de Elcano, to seize the Spice Islands. Their expedition was instructed to consolidate the Spanish hold on the lands Magellan had claimed, to determine the best trade route between the islands of the Pacific and America, and to find and annex the Great Southern Continent. As vast as the expedition's charge were the disasters that it encountered. With seven ships and 450 men, the armada could not locate Magellan's strait. Loaysa and Elcano lost three ships before they found the strait, and three more were lost in the four months it took for the expedition to pass through to the Pacific. Only the *Santa María de la Victoria* remained to cross the ocean, and on the way both Loaysa and Elcano died. Crewman Martin Carquisano piloted the *Santa María* to Guam and then to the Moluccas.

Arriving at Tidore in early 1527, the once-mighty armada, now consisting of one ship and only 115 men, took on the Portuguese. Hernán Cortés, the governor of New Spain (Mexico), had been instructed earlier by the Council of the Indies to send a fleet from Mexico to aid Loaysa and Elcano as they seized the Moluccas. Only one ship from this fleet, the *Florida,* reached Tidore. When its captain, Álvaro de Saavedra Cerón, learned that Loaysa and Elcano were dead and saw how outnumbered the Spanish were, he resolved to go back to Mexico for reinforcements in June 1528. A handful of his men joined the survivors of the Loaysa-Elcano expedition, and, aided by the native Moluccans, who hated the Portuguese invaders, Spain undertook a guerilla campaign against Portugal until Saavedra returned with more gunships.

Saavedra was immediately blown off course as he tried to sail back across the Pacific. His ship was driven south, to the coast of New Guinea. Saavedra became the first European to walk on its shores. Saavedra made another mighty effort to sail into winds that would carry him back to Mexico, but he died in the attempt. Although the *Florida* did find islands in the Admiralty and Marshall groups, it was leaking badly and the crew decided to return to the Moluccas. The *Florida* arrived at Tidore in late December 1529 and fell to pieces. Its crew and the survivors of the *Santa María* were stranded in the Spice Islands. Unbeknownst to them, half a world away their king had made their struggles irrelevant by selling his claim to the islands to Portugal for 350,000 ducats.

SPAIN GAINS A NEW RULER AND A PACIFIC COLONY

Emperor Charles V was forced to sacrifice his claims on the Moluccas to pay for an expensive war with France. Plus, there were other expenses to be met. As the Holy Roman Emperor, Charles ruled Austria and needed to raise money to defend it against the Turks. Gold and silver began to pour into Spain as conquistador Francisco Pizarro undertook the destruction of the Inca Empire in Peru. In the 1530s and 1540s, Charles invested in the sure wealth of South America rather than squander any more investments in the Pacific. He did use his bases to send an expedition to the Islands of Lazarus in 1543. The only result of this expedition was that the islands were renamed the Philippines in honor of the 16-year-old heir to the throne of Spain, Don Felipé.

Worn out at the age of 55, Charles abdicated in favor of Philip in 1556. Philip II inherited all of Charles's possessions. They were vast: Spain, the Americas, parts of France, much of Italy, the Netherlands, and northern Africa. Philip also inherited Charles's debts

Founded by Spain in the late 16th century, Manila developed as an important trading port. This early 20th-century photograph shows boats along the Pasig River in Manila, the capital of the Philippines. *(Library of Congress, Prints and Photographs Division [LC-USZC4-3231])*

and enemies. French privateers were menacing the treasure ships bound for Spain from America. The Casa de Contratación ordered all merchant ships to sail in convoys protected by galleons. Philip also knew the French had sent explorer Jacques Cartier to America in search of a northern passage to the Pacific in the 1540s. Philip knew the fortunes of his empire rested on his ability to establish a powerful presence in the Pacific. He chose the Philippines as the base from which Spain's influence would spread. The Philippines were also close enough to China to become a major port of trade. Spain's sailors had amply demonstrated they could cross the Pacific,

but it remained to be proven if they could sail back.

The ports of South America's west coast proved valuable as staging grounds for Spain's new thrust into the Pacific. In November 1564, Andrés Urdaneta, a Spanish soldier, and Miguel López de Legazpi, an administrator in New Spain, left Mexico with six gunships and 350 men. Their goal was to establish an armed base in the Philippines. When their ships reached Cebu in April of the next year, the Spanish built a fort and began to move through the neighboring islands, informing their inhabitants that they were now subjects of King Philip. In June 1565, Urdaneta returned to Mexico to summon more men and ships. By sailing farther north than any previous captain had attempted, Urdaneta became the first navigator to successfully make an east-west voyage across the Pacific.

Manila quickly became a great trading port, just as Philip had hoped. Silks, pearls, precious gems, and rare woods from China were exchanged for the gold and silver of South America's mines. By the 1570s, every January fleet, called the Annual Galleon, sailed from Acapulco. Sailing with the trade winds, the fleet could reach Manila in as few as 80 days. The ships would be loaded with valuable goods from China and Southeast Asia. When the monsoon winds began in June, the Galleon would follow the route charted by Urdaneta as far north as the Marianas Islands and then proceed east to the coast of California. The coastal currents off California would speed ships back to Acapulco. The Galleon could make the entire trip in six months.

TERRA AUSTRALIS INCOGNITA

With his grasp on the Philippines firmly established, Philip turned his attention to the discovery of the great southern land Marco Polo had described. The Spanish were convinced the legendary gold mines of the Bible's King Solomon would be found somewhere on this Terra Australis Incognita. In November 1567 two ships, the *Todos Santos* and *Los Reyes,* were sent from the Peruvian port of Callao to find and claim the southland. Álvaro de Mendaña de Neyra commanded the expeditionary force of 70 soldiers and sailors, four priests, and 80 Peruvian slaves.

Unsure of his course, Mendaña sailed between the Tuamotus and the Marquesas without seeing them. Mendaña's ships sailed for more than 6,000 miles without seeing any land other than Tuvalu, which was deemed too small and barren to offer sustenance to the starving crew. Finally, they sighted land on February 7, 1568. Canoes paddled out to meet the ships. The Spanish were afraid of the men who approached. Their dark skin appeared almost black, and their teeth were filed to sharp points. They also carried spears and daggers. Mendaña appeased the warriors with trade goods, and a small boat was sent from the *Todos Santos* to the shore. The Spanish planted a cross, claimed the new land for Philip, and named it Santa Ysabel. They were sure they had found the Great Southern Continent.

Mendaña and his men spent six months trading with the people of Santa Ysabel and exploring the region in a brigantine they built and christened the *Santiago*. It was soon clear that Santa Ysabel was an island, not a continent. Still, as the Spanish encountered and named islands such as Guadalcanal and San Cristobal, Mendaña clung to his belief that Terra Australis Incognita was close by. His men were not so certain and were beginning to grow wary of the region's people. The priests were not successful in their conversion attempts. Violent encounters were growing frequent, and even gestures of peace were repulsive to the Spanish. Mendaña's men had met one of the very few Pacific cultures that practiced ritual cannibalism. When they were offered the severed arm and shoulder of a child, the Spanish were disgusted and quietly buried the body parts with a Christian ceremony.

Mendaña decided to set sail in mid-August. The expedition followed the northern route to California, passing the Marshall Islands and Wake Island. But the way was not smooth. Provisions ran short, and the crew was limited to one pint of water and a bit of bread each day. The *Todos Santos*

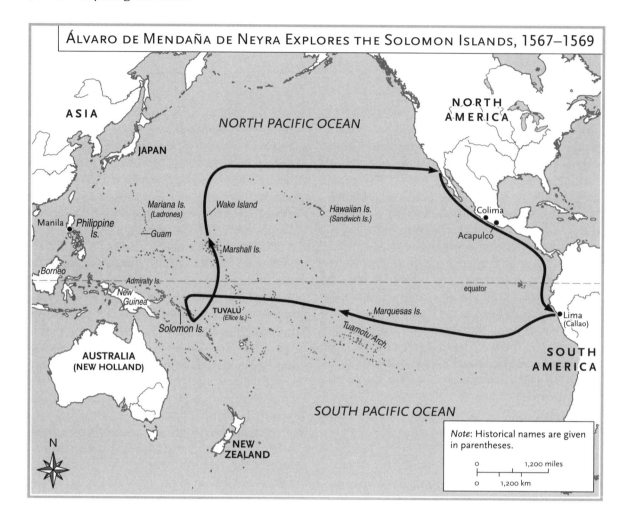

ÁLVARO DE MENDAÑA DE NEYRA EXPLORES THE SOLOMON ISLANDS, 1567–1569

ASIA

NORTH PACIFIC OCEAN

NORTH AMERICA

JAPAN

Mariana Is. (Ladrones)

Wake Island

Hawaiian Is. (Sandwich Is.)

Colima

Manila

Philippine Is.

Guam

Acapulco

Borneo

Marshall Is.

Admiralty Is.

equator

New Guinea

TUVALU (Ellice Is.)

Marquesas Is.

Lima (Callao)

Solomon Is.

Tuamotu Arch.

AUSTRALIA (NEW HOLLAND)

SOUTH AMERICA

SOUTH PACIFIC OCEAN

N

NEW ZEALAND

Note: Historical names are given in parentheses.

0   1,200 miles

0   1,200 km

disappeared. The other ship, *Los Reyes,* nearly capsized in a storm. Huge gaps opened in its hull, and it turned on its side. The mast had to be cut away to right it. Even when the ship was righted and a mast improvised, the crew was in peril. Men died from starvation as *Los Reyes* slowly sailed east. There was no water and no rain. Mendaña was threatened with mutiny. Just as hope for survival was about to extinguished, a log was spotted floating near the ship. It had no barnacles on it, which meant that land must be near.

Four months after leaving Santa Ysabel, *Los Reyes* made the coast of Baja California and put into the port of Colima. One week later, the *Todos Santos* appeared. Mendaña ordered the arrest of its captain, Pedro Sarmiento de Gamboa, on charges of insubordination. After repairing his ships at Colima, Mendaña sailed to Callao in September 1569 to report his discoveries to the Spanish officials there. They were unimpressed. Mendaña had been sent to find the Great Southern Continent and had failed. An official changed the name of the Santa Ysabel islands to the Solomons, pointedly emphasizing his disappointment by sarcastically referring to the biblical king and his fabled gold mines.

THREATS TO SPANISH WEALTH AND POWER

New challenges to Spain's control of the Pacific appeared in the 1570s. English privateers like Francis Drake posed a serious threat to the Annual Galleon. Drake was born about 1542 to a Protestant family during the reign of the Catholic Queen Mary, who was known as Bloody Mary for her relentless persecution of English Protestants. Filled with hatred of the Spanish, who had supported the Catholic Mary (also wife of their king, Philip), Drake went to sea at an early age. He sailed on raiding ships in the Caribbean and earned the nickname given to him by the Spanish—El Draque ("the dragon").

In 1572, Drake was given a privateering assignment to hunt treasure ships off the eastern coast of Central America, called the Spanish Main. So successful was this mission that a group of investors commissioned Drake to conduct a more extensive raiding mission in South America. Anxious to avoid the appearance of inciting a war with Spain, Queen Elizabeth I would not grant letters of marque and reprisal to the expedition of five ships, but it is likely that she secretly invested in the enterprise. Essentially a pirate, Drake sailed for South America on December 13, 1577, in command of the lead vessel, the *Pelican.*

The expedition did not have a fortunate start. Drake put down a mutiny attempt at Port St. Julían, burying the leader of the attempt, Thomas Doughty, under the gibbets that had hung the corpses of Ferdinand Magellan's mutineers. Of the five ships, only Drake's, renamed the *Golden Hind,* reached Pacific waters. Two were scuttled, with their crews and supplies transferred to the other ships. One disappeared in the violent seas of Cape Horn. The last returned to England. The *Golden Hind* sailed up the west coast of South America, raiding Spanish ships and settlements. Off Lima in June 1579, Drake found the booty he had sought. The *Golden Hind* captured the Spanish ship *Cacafuego.* Drake's crew worked four days to load the Spanish treasure—a dozen chests of silver

Francis Drake was the first captain to circumnavigate the world and survive the journey. *(Library of Congress, Prints and Photographs Division [LC-USZ62-121191])*

coins, 26 tons of silver in bar form, 80 pounds of gold, and unimagined quantities of gems—onto the *Golden Hind.* One historian estimates that the expedition's investors yielded a 4,700 percent return on their investment.

Although he commanded an unsanctioned expedition, Drake had probably been

Cape Horn, shown in this photograph, is located on the southernmost tip of South America. *(National Archives of Canada)*

asked by the Crown to further explore the coast of the Americas, to search for a northern passage across North America, and to discover new territory for England. Raiding Spanish posts as he went, Drake sailed the *Golden Hind* north from Peru. When he reached present-day San Francisco, Drake claimed northern California, which he named New Albion, for England. After refitting the ship and replenishing supplies in New Albion, the expedition may have sailed as far north as Alaska. If Drake did have a secret assignment, that would explain why Drake did not keep a log of the expedition and why he chose to cross the Pacific to return home to England.

Well provisioned and using charts captured from the Spanish, Drake and his men sailed easily across 6,000 miles of open ocean. The *Golden Hind* added to its cargo, and its treasure, with the purchase of six tons of cloves in the Moluccas. When the ship arrived in England on September 26, 1580, Drake was celebrated as England's greatest hero, pirate though he was. Drake had brought back the riches of Spain and the riches of the Spice Islands. The next year he was knighted by Queen Elizabeth I, taking as his motto, *Sic Parva Magna* ("from small beginnings, greatness").

Just after Drake returned from the Spice Islands, the Moluccas at last came under Spanish rule. In 1581, Philip claimed the crown of Portugal and sovereignty over its Pacific territories. The long-sought prize was balanced by the impending loss of the Netherlands. An armed rebellion by the Dutch demanded Philip's attention and treasury. England, emboldened by Drake's victories, was poised to go to war against Spain. In 1588 the English defeated Philip's armada. Neighboring France was no ally, and Catholic Spain was increasingly at war with Protestant Europe. To Philip, the quest for the great southern land then became an opportunity to expand the reach of Catholicism.

SPIRITUAL CONQUEST AND THE SEARCH FOR THE SOUTH LAND

For 20 years Mendaña had been petitioning the crown to send him to settle a colony in the Solomons. In 1595, Philip agreed to the plan. Mendaña went to Peru to organize his expedition. Four ships were outfitted to carry the usual crew of sailors, soldiers, and priests. But when the ships left Callao in April they also carried colonists—men, women, and children. Mendaña's own wife, Ysabel, came with him.

On July 21, Mendaña announced they had arrived in the Solomons. But the people of the islands looked very different from those Mendaña had met on his previous voyage. They had lighter skin, and many had intricate tattoos over much of their bodies. Mendaña named the islands the Marquesas, in honor of the viceroy of Peru. While interactions between the islanders and Mendaña's people were initially friendly, within two weeks the Marquesans had grown tired of their guests' arrogance and dependence. The Spanish, in turn, resented continual looting by the islanders. The chief pilot of the expedition, Pedro Fernández de Quirós, reported that after two weeks on the island, the Spanish were shooting its inhabitants for fun and that perhaps as many as 200 islanders had been killed.

When Mendaña's ships left the Marquesas, they became lost. Mendaña seemed to have forgotten his way to the Solomons. His sailors threatened mutiny in September just before the ships came to an island group that looked like the Solomons to Mendaña. The inhabitants

Slaves, Women, and Colonists

Ships crossing the pacific had more diverse crews than one might think. Several African men worked on Ferdinand Magellan's ships, although it is not clear whether they were servants or slaves. Two black servants, Richmond and Dorlton, served as naturalist Joseph Banks's personal servants on the *Endeavour*. In the 19th century, many whaling ships had free black sailors on board. In 1595, Doña Ysabel Barreto Mendaña accompanied her husband on his search for the Solomon Islands and, after his death, assumed the governorship of the short-lived colony of Santa Cruz.

She led, briefly, one of the many contingents of people sent to settle permanently on Pacific Islands. These settlements, such as those established by Spain in the Philippines during the 1560s, were intended to service trading vessels crossing the Pacific from South America. The colonists' success also strengthened the claims of European nations to ownership of particular islands and territories.

The first woman to circumnavigate the globe, Jeanne Baret, did so disguised as a man. In 1766 she sailed on the French ship *Bodeuse* as servant to its naturalist, Philibert Commerson, and was probably his lover. Her ruse went undetected by the rest of the crew and by its commander, Louis-Antoine de Bougainville, for most of the voyage. When the *Bodeuse* landed in Tahiti, the Tahitians identified Baret as a woman.

of the islands also looked liked the people of the Solomons. But they did not understand Mendaña when he spoke to them in the language he had learned more than 20 years before. He named the islands Santa Cruz, and they were 300 miles east of the Solomons. The clans on the islands were at war, and the Spanish were caught in the hostilities. Nonetheless, Mendaña decided to establish the first colony there. After a month the colonists threatened to overthrow Mendaña, who was now very ill with malaria. Mendaña's wife, Ysabel, persuaded him to execute the captain of the soldiers, who she saw as the plot's ringleader. The military commander was beheaded, along with two of his soldiers. Mendaña had the heads displayed on poles and ordered the colonists to attend a Mass celebrated on the

bloodied ground. The colonists' situation became even worse when a Spanish soldier killed the island chief, Malope. On October 15, while outraged islanders besieged his colonists, Mendaña died of malaria.

Pilot Pedro Fernández de Quirós now took charge of the expedition, although Mendaña's wife assumed the governance of the colony. Malaria was rampant among the colonists. They knew the murder of Malope would not be forgiven. Quirós determined to lead the colonists to safety. On November 18 the colonists gratefully boarded the ships. Quirós knew that his rotting vessels would never make it to the Solomons and, even if they did, they needed extensive repairs that could be done only in an established port. He directed the ships to the Philippines. Only one, the *San*

Jeronimo, arrived in Manila in February 1596. Before the year was out, Quirós returned to South America. He was to spend the next five years trying to return to the Pacific.

When Quirós reached Spain in 1600, he learned that King Philip II had died two years before. His son, King Philip III, now ruled and was burdened by his father's debts. The entire budget of Spain was 9.7 million ducats, and half of that was spent to reduce the debt of 68 million ducats left by Philip II. Spain clearly did not have the money to support Quirós's grand plan to conquer the Pacific. Because Quirós was determined not simply to win ter-

ritory for Spain but also to win souls for the Catholic Church, he journeyed to Rome to enlist the pope in his plan. Pope Clement VIII supported Quirós and wrote an order directing the Spanish authorities to undertake the mission.

Not until 1605 did Quirós assemble his three ships and crew of 300 soldiers and sailors in Callao. He enlisted four priests, but no women or children joined the expedition. Quirós had learned on his last Pacific venture that Spain would have to subdue and Christianize the people of the Pacific before European settlement could be initiated. Quirós

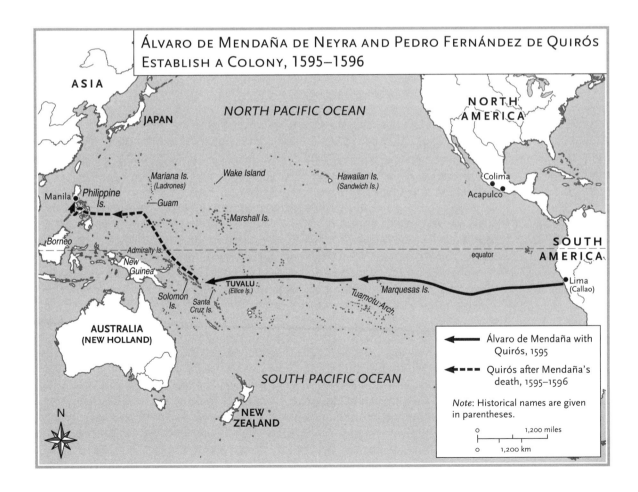

was also determined that this expedition would not suffer from hunger and thirst. His cargo included seedlings, fruit trees, farm animals, and a device for distilling fresh water from saltwater. Instead of wooden casks that rotted and spoiled water, the ships carried clay water jars.

To emphasize the religious purpose of the expedition, when the ships left Callao on December 21, 1605, Quirós and his officers wore monks' habits. Pilot González de Leza wrote, "We sailed with good will to serve God and spread out Holy Faith, and to bring credit to the King our Lord." Quirós instituted a strict moral order. There was to be no swearing or blaspheming on his ships. All cards and dice were thrown overboard, and the crew was expected to attend Mass daily. Moreover, Quirós was resolved to avoid the violence and bloodshed that previous Spanish expeditions had visited upon the native people of the Pacific.

Anxious not to repeat Mendaña's error in missing the Solomons entirely, Quirós sailed in

Sixteenth-Century Ships and Navigation

Spain's domination of the Pacific in the 16th century depended on great advances in shipbuilding and navigational technology. In the early part of the century, most ships sailing in Pacific waters were carracks. Larger and sturdier than the caravels that had carried early expeditions, like that of Columbus, the carrack had a U-shaped hull and three or four masts rigged with square sails. These features made the carrack faster, able to travel farther and steadier, and able to withstand the storms of the southern ocean.

By the middle of the 16th century, galleons became the standard ship for both Spanish and English expeditions. The galleon was more maneuverable than the carrack, with its slimmer profile and almost flat hull. Its low center of gravity made it able to carry more guns and more cargo. The great silver and gold shipping route between Spain's possessions in America and its ports in the Philippines was plied on galleons.

European sailors had been able to calculate the position of their ship's latitude since the ninth century. They did so by measuring the height of the sun using an astrolabe, or of the Northern Star using a cross staff or a quadrant. But they could not accurately measure longitude, though the geographer Ptolemy had introduced the concept in the second century A.D.

Through a process called dead reckoning, navigators were able to get a rough idea of longitude. Dead reckoning depended on measuring a ship's speed, which was the distance traveled over a specific period of time. One method of measurement, the log line, gave the term *knot* to the unit of nautical speed. A rope with knots tied at regular spaces was thrown over the side of the ship. The navigator counted the number of knots the ship passed as sand ran through an hourglass to figure out how fast the ship was sailing. Once speed a zigzag pattern, covering a broad reach of the ocean. Still, the waters the expedition sailed through seemed empty of islands. The crew, led by chief pilot Juan Ochoa de Bilboa, attempted mutiny because they found Quirós's piety and strict rules oppressive. Searching for a place to replenish dwindling water supplies because the expedition had run out of fuel for the distiller, in early February the ships anchored at Hao in the Tuamotus. Quirós christened one of these islands, possibly Raroia, La Sagitaria. On April 7, 1606, the ships arrived at Taumako. In spite of Quirós's pledge of kindness to native peoples, the Taumakans were forced at gunpoint to supply the ships with water and food. The islanders told Quirós of an island five days west. He was sure they were describing one of the Solomon Islands. He was also told of a massive land to the south and was equally sure that must be Terra Australis Incognita. Four islanders were taken hostage to serve as guides.

On April 29 the ships approached a large island. Certain he had discovered the Great

was determined, a navigator could calculate how far his ship had sailed from shore or from a previous position. A ship's compass indicated the ship's direc-

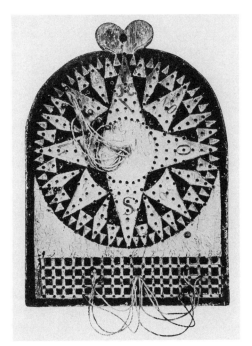

tion. Knowing the distance traveled and the direction taken, the navigator could chart the new position. Navigators and mapmakers depended on knowing a ship's course over the months of a voyage. The course was simply the ship's position, measured with the log line and compass, during a span of time. Position needed to be entered into a ship's log (journal) every day. Sailors, who would take the measurements during their watch (a four-hour shift), were usually illiterate. They used a traverse board, inserting pegs into holes to record compass direction and knot speed, to make a record of the ship's course. An officer could then "read" the traverse board and write an entry for the watch in the ship's log. Since neither 16th-century magnetic compasses nor log-line measurements were exact, expeditions frequently went off course by hundreds of miles.

Sailors used the pegs and holes of a traverse board to record compass direction and knot speed. *(National Archives of Canada)*

Southern Continent, Quirós decided to plant his colony on its fertile land. The expedition had found neither the Solomons nor a continent. The island was in the New Hebrides, now known as Vanuatu. Quirós named the island New Jerusalem and appointed Luis Vaez de Torres as camp master, directing him to build a fort and a church for a new settlement. Because the inhabitants of the island threatened the Spanish settlers, Quirós created a Ministry of War and Marine. By this point Quirós was ill with malaria. His fevers caused delusions, but the men obeyed because his power as commander was absolute. He created an elaborate ritual in which the men were initiated into a religious order, the Knights of the Holy Ghost. In another rite, Quirós claimed the "continent" for Spain. He christened it Australia del Espíritu Santo to honor his king, who ruled Austria as well as Spain.

As quickly as Quirós had decided to settle on Espíritu Santo, he decided to leave. Rambling speeches had convinced his crew that he was crazy, and continual attacks from the native Vanuatuans had convinced the priests that it was impossible to convert the "devils." Quirós told his men that they would go west to Santa Cruz. But once the ships got underway, the commander changed his mind and turned back for Espíritu Santo. Stormy seas blew the *San Pedro y Paulo,* with Quirós aboard, out to sea. Separated from his expedition, Quirós searched fruitlessly for Santa Cruz. The *San Pedro y Paulo* crossed the Pacific to Mexico and arrived in Acapulco in November 1606.

With the loss of Quirós and the *San Pedro y Paulo,* Luix Vaez de Torres took command of the expedition. The *San Pedrico* and the *Los Tres Reyes* searched for Quirós, but to no avail. During the search Torres did establish that Espíritu Santo was an island, not a continent. Before the expedition left Callao, the viceroy of Peru had given Torres a set of sealed orders,

to be opened in the event that Quirós died or if the ships separated. The orders directed Torres to search for the southern continent as far to the south as 1,200 miles below the equator. Torres left Vanuatu and sailed to 21° south latitude, farther than the orders specified. He did not find any land, but he did note that the weather became increasingly cold the farther south he sailed.

Torres had completed his assigned orders. With no specific instructions from the viceroy, Torres decided to explore a land that Inigo Ortiz de Retes had discovered in 1545. Ortiz had claimed New Guinea for Spain, but geographers had little information about its position or size. No one knew if New Guinea was an island or part of the Great Southern continent. Torres intended to explore the northern coast of New Guinea and then take his ships to the Philippines. Headwinds prevented Torres from reaching the northern coast. Instead, his ships entered the shallows to the south. Slowly, Torres sailed through treacherous reefs and shark-infested waters, charting his route so carefully that it is still used by shipping traffic. The expedition was a scant hundred miles from the northern coast of Australia, and Torres might have seen its Cape York. When Torres came to open water, he knew that he had proved New Guinea to be an island. He had also charted the strait that today bears his name.

From Muslim missionaries he met at the western tip of New Guinea, Torres learned he was only 200 miles from the Moluccas. His ships sailed to Ternate, where Torres left *Los Tres Reyes.* Aboard the *San Pedrico,* Torres arrived in Manila on May 26, 1607. There he learned that Quirós had returned to Spain with grandiose descriptions of the continent he had discovered. Quirós prepared more than 50 memorials, documents meant to persuade the authorities to sponsor him for another expedition. He described a land so

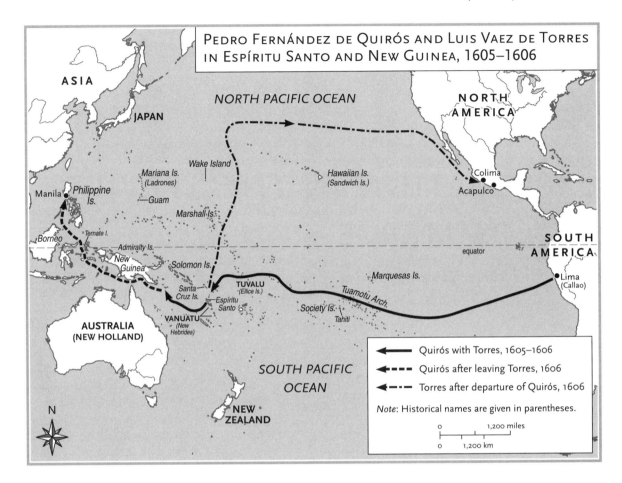

PEDRO FERNÁNDEZ DE QUIRÓS AND LUIS VAEZ DE TORRES IN ESPÍRITU SANTO AND NEW GUINEA, 1605–1606

large that 200,000 colonists could be supported by its fertile soil. Quirós recommended the friendly native people as prospective Christians. It was a land where no one got sick and where fish and meat stayed fresh for two days. From Manila, Torres wrote letters that campaigned against Quirós and testified to his fanatical behavior on Espíritu Santo. Quirós spent seven years attempting to mount an expedition and died penniless and friendless in Cuba, on his way to Peru to find a ship.

Even if Quirós had been of entirely sound mind, it was unlikely that the Spanish Crown could have supported another major effort in the Pacific by 1614. The days in which the Pacific was referred to as the Spanish Lake were over. Spain never recovered its naval strength after the defeat of its armada by England in 1588. Although its colonies in America brought over 7 million ducats annually to Spain's treasury, Philip III had used the steady revenue as collateral for loans that further weakened the Spanish economy. As the national debt increased, so too did its annual deficit. A high inflation rate only rendered Spain more vulnerable. The first decade of the 17th century proved to be the twilight of Spanish control of the Pacific.

6

EXPLORATION IN THE SERVICE OF COMMERCE

King Philip II of Spain sowed the seeds of Dutch success in the Pacific. When Philip assumed the throne of Portugal and possession of the Moluccas in 1581, Spain was trying to put down a rebellion in the Netherlands. Philip outlawed trade between Lisbon and the Netherlands, hoping to ruin the Dutch economy and so end the Netherlands's quest for independence from Spanish rule. Dutch demand for spices was traditionally strong, and the Netherlands had been a major market for the goods of the East. The ban on trade with Portugal encouraged the Dutch to undertake a massive smuggling operation. Dutch shipping firms contracted with other European nations, principally England, to carry cargo on their ships. Privateers raided ships returning to Spain and Portugal from the Moluccas and India. These "Sea Beggars" took advantage of the destruction of Philip's navy by the English in 1588 and were able to gain control of the northern coast of Europe.

Dutch trading vessels craftily evaded Spanish warships at Gibraltar and so established trade with Italy and Constantinople. Ships sailed between Amsterdam and the west coast of Africa, and Spain's naval forces were too weak to intercept them. Spain was losing markets for its cargos of spices at this time. Tastes had changed in the countries around the Mediterranean, and customers preferred sugar from the West Indies to spices from the Moluccas. In Northern Europe, spices were in high demand. Dutch smugglers and privateers found a ready market for their goods in Germany, Russia, and the Scandinavian countries. Martin Luther, the German Protestant leader, remarked that Germans bought more spices than grain.

The Dutch economy boomed, and by 1590 more than 3,000 ships, most capable of ocean voyaging, were anchored in the ports of the Netherlands. In 1595, nine Dutch merchants formed the Company of the Far Lands and sent four ships, swift sturdy *jachts* and *fluyts*, far better than any ships previously sailing east, to the Spice Islands. Commanded by Cornelis de Houtman, the flotilla rounded the Cape of Good Hope and reached the Moluccas to find a warm welcome from the Moluccans, who continued to resent the Portuguese. Houtman returned with a fortune in peppercorns. The Dutch determined to wrestle control of the spice trade. In 1598, Oliver Van Noort was sent to capture and destroy Spanish and Portuguese ships in the East. Van Noort sailed west through the Strait of Magellan, battled the Spanish in the Philippines, escaped near-destruction, and sailed back to the Netherlands around the Cape of Good Hope.

THE DUTCH EAST INDIA COMPANY

Van Noort's circumnavigation increased Dutch confidence in establishing a regular trade to the East. By 1601, 65 Dutch ships had voyaged to the Moluccas. The government of the Netherlands, the States-General, ruled that the best way to maximize profits would be to coordinate trading efforts. But the government did not retain the power to conduct and regulate trade for itself, as Emperor Charles V had done in Spain. Instead, in 1602 it granted a charter to the Verenigde Oostindische Companie (Dutch East India Company), which became known all over the world simply by its initials, V. O. C. A joint stock company, it was controlled by a board of directors, and anyone could buy shares. This company was granted a monopoly on trade to the East. Only navigators and shipping companies licensed by the V. O. C. could ply the waters of the East Indies. The States-General granted the company unprecedented power. The V. O. C. could enter treaties, create ports, establish governments for its possessions, and

determine laws and punishments. It could coin money, establish an army, and wage war against its enemies.

The Dutch East India Company could also finance expeditions to find new territories for the Netherlands, new lands that could prove to be rich in trade goods like spices and gold. Stories about New Guinea circulated among sailors. Some told of brief sightings of a vast land to its south. Geographers speculated that this land was Terra Australis Incognita. The V. O. C. was eager to claim it for the Netherlands and instructed its trading ships to watch for the elusive southland.

In 1605 the company's headquarters at Bantam in the Cocos Islands provided Willem Janz with the ship *Duyfken*. Officials directed Janz to explore New Guinea and to search for Terra Australis Incognita. Janz sailed along 900 miles of New Guinea's southern coast. He had nothing to report to the V. O. C. about trading prospects in this region; it appeared wild and barren of gold. Janz then turned south and soon sighted land. Because he had not passed all the way through Torres Strait—the charts Luis Vaez de Torres had so carefully made long remained a Spanish secret—Janz assumed this land was part of New Guinea. In fact, it was the northern coast of the Australian continent. He sent men ashore to find water, and they reported that the land was dry and wild, inhabited by naked savages. When Janz reported to Bantam in June 1606 he recommended against further investment in exploring the land he called New Holland.

By the first decade of the 17th century, the Dutch East India Company dominated the East as it set out to control trade to Europe. Although peace between Spain and the Netherlands had been negotiated in 1609, the two nations remained in a virtual war in the Pacific Ocean far longer. With its resilient and fast

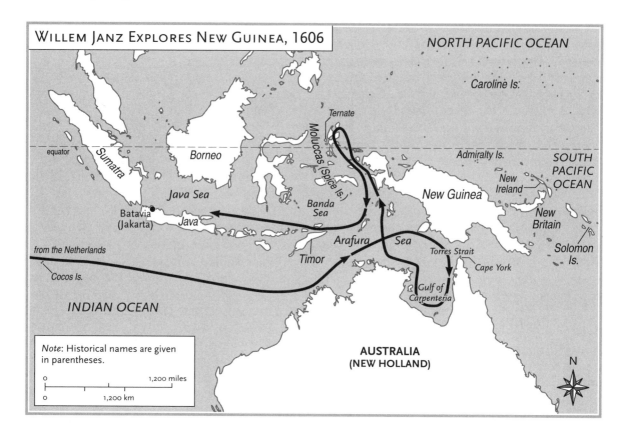

WILLEM JANZ EXPLORES NEW GUINEA, 1606

NORTH PACIFIC OCEAN

Caroline Is.

Ternate

equator

Sumatra

Borneo

Moluccas (Spice Is.)

Admiralty Is.

SOUTH PACIFIC OCEAN

New Guinea

New Ireland

New Britain

Java Sea

Java

Banda Sea

Solomon Is.

Batavia (Jakarta)

Arafura   Sea

Torres Strait

from the Netherlands

Timor

Cape York

Cocos Is.

Gulf of Carpenteria

INDIAN OCEAN

Note: Historical names are given in parentheses.

0   1,200 miles

0   1,200 km

AUSTRALIA
(NEW HOLLAND)

N

ships, sophisticated armaments, experienced sailors, accurate charts, and modern instruments, the V. O. C. was able to evict the Spanish and Portuguese from most of the important ports of the East. With the Moluccas under firm control, the Dutch expanded their reach to India's Malabar Coast and even to Japan. Spain managed to retain the Philippines, and Portugal held on to Macao in China and Goa in India, but the Dutch still impeded their ships from actually reaching the ports. Article 34 of the Dutch East India Company charter decreed that no ships without licenses could sail east of the Cape of Good Hope or west of the Strait of Magellan. Company privateers would harass Spanish and Portuguese traders, furthering the decline of their Pacific hopes.

ISAAC LE MAIRE CHALLENGES THE MONOPOLY

Even some Dutch found the V. O. C. monopoly oppressive. Isaac Le Maire, who had been a director of the company, was one of them. Le Maire had read of a speculation by Francis Drake that a passage to the Pacific might exist below Tierra del Fuego. Moreover, the lands that Drake had seen to his south might be the Great Southern Continent. Le Maire hired Willem Schouten, a pilot who had long sailed in the Pacific for the V. O. C., to search for the rumored passage and to find the continent. Le Maire appointed his son Jakob commander of the expedition to protect his interests. In

Cartography

Cartography is the science and art of mapmaking. Cartography played an integral role in the exploration of the Pacific, from the stick charts of the Polynesian voyagers to the elaborate maps of New Zealand that resulted from Cook's explorations of its coast. The earliest maps carried by Portuguese and Spanish expeditions were called *portolanos*. Drawn on goatskins that could withstand moisture, and only roughly depicting coastlines, portolanos were not very accurate. Their makers really did not know much about the geography of the new regions, and they also did not know how to show the curve of the Earth's surface on a flat map.

The first maps of the whole world appeared in the early 16th century. Gerardus Mercator (1512–94) was the first cartographer to devise an accurate way to portray the curve of the Earth. Mercator's cylindrical projection is still used in many nautical maps and on globes. A bit of a historical mystery, the first map to show the as-yet-unnamed Pacific Ocean was produced in 1507 by the Dutch mapmaker Martin Waldseemüller. This was six years before Vasco Núñez Balboa's sighting of the ocean. Waldseemüller was probably influenced by Amerigo Vespucci's discoveries in the Americas and so speculatively emphasized the idea that a new continent had been discovered by depicting it embraced by vast oceans on both sides.

By the 17th century, as a result of the explosion of exploration and advances in mathematics, maps were much more accurate. Many of these maps included careful illustrations of a region's plants, animals, and people, along with physical features of the coasts and land. Maps were an important way for ordinary people to learn about newly explored and acquired territories. So important were good maps to imperial efforts that several nations, including the United States, undertook national mapping projects in the 18th and 19th centuries.

June 1615 the *Hoorn* and the *Eendracht* left Holland. As they sailed along the coast of Africa, the men began to show signs of scurvy. The ships put into a port in Sierra Leone and traded beads and knives for 25,000 lemons, which they dried and stored for the voyage and which helped explain the low incidence of death from scurvy during the rest of the expedition.

In December, as the *Hoorn* and the *Eendracht* coasted along Patagonia, the *Hoorn* caught fire. The men had just enough time to transfer its provisions, guns, and anchors to the *Eendracht* before the ship was consumed. Down to one ship, the expedition sailed past Cape Virgenes and passed the opening of Magellan's strait on January 24, 1616. The air was turning frigid. Penguins lined the shores, and the crew watched seals cavorting in the *Eendracht*'s wake. Land was sighted, a large mass. Schouten became worried. It might be that the southern American continent extended much farther than he had thought, that there was no passage to the Pacific besides the Strait of Magellan. But the sea turned dark as the *Eendracht* struggled through bigger and bigger swells. Schouten realized the landmass was indeed an island, which he named Staten Land, and that his ship had entered a strait. On January 26, the *Eendracht* rounded a rocky headland that Le Maire named for the lost ship, Cape Hoorn. He wrote in his diary that day about seeing the waters change from dark green to very deep blue as the ship entered the Pacific, "whereat we were glad, holding that a way had been discovered by us hitherto unknown to man."

Sailing northwest, the *Eendracht* encountered no land until April 10, when the islands of the Tuamotus came into view. The people on the island had experienced rough treatment by Spanish and Portuguese ships and did not paddle their canoes out to greet the ships. "Eventually we sent our shallops [rowboats] ashore with eight musketeers and six men with swords," wrote Le Maire, "in order to see what there was on the island and to make friends with them." The islanders apparently did not find the weapons very friendly and attacked the Dutch landing party. "There were women among the Indians who fell upon the men's necks and shrieked, though our people did not know what this means." No one on either side was killed, but Schouten thought it best to weigh anchor and find provisions on another island.

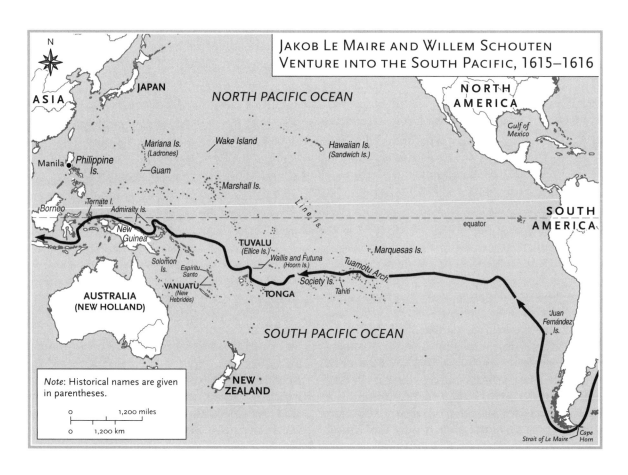

POULAHO, KING of the FRIENDLY ISLANDS, drinking KAVA.

Created by John Webber, an artist on one of James Cook's voyages, this image shows Poulaho, a native king, seated in a public house before his people who have come to visit him. The man prostrate before Poulaho is kissing his feet. In the background, one of the people prepares kava, a potent drink made from chewed pepper plants from which the drink is named. *(National Archives of Canada)*

As the *Eendracht* sailed farther into the Pacific during May, its crew saw a great *vaataie,* a double-hulled canoe, and followed it to its home island, Tafahi in Tonga. From Tonga the expedition sailed north and came to beautiful volcanic islands they named *Hoorn.* The ship was a thousand miles below the equator, anchored off Futuna and Alofi. The men of the *Eendracht* rested two weeks on the islands, trading cloth, metal pots, fishhooks, and other European goods for food and water. At night the Dutch would entertain the islanders with trumpets and drums, and the islanders would dance and sing for the sailors. But the islanders were offended when the Dutch refused to share their *kava,* a potent drink made from chewed pepper plants. The *Een-dracht* had overstayed its welcome. "As we sat at table we gave the savages to understand that we would be leaving in two days' time," reads Le Maire's journal. "Whereat the king was so pleased that he at once leaped to his feet and shouted that we should soon be going. At this there was much rejoicing."

Le Maire was certain that the *Eendracht* was close to the Solomons, and therefore close to what he argued, based on the records made by Quirós, was the Great Southern Continent. Schouten was unsure whether the *Eendracht* would be seaworthy for many more months of exploration. Schouten's plan to sail to the Moluccas was adopted, and the *Eendracht* sailed from the Hoorn Islands on the first of June. Three weeks later the lookout excitedly shouted that he saw land stretching far north and south just ahead of the ship. Warriors in canoes rushed to attack the ship, and the *Eendracht* encountered much hostility as they made the first European landings on New Ireland. By August the expedition was north of New Guinea, able to carry on amicable trade with its people, who were accustomed to Europeans and their ships.

September saw the *Eendracht* in the Moluccas, where it took on a cargo of cloves at Ternate. When Le Maire and Schouten arrived in the booming harbor of Batavia in Java, officials of the Dutch East India Company seized the *Eendracht* and its cargo. The expedition's leaders were considered criminals in a port ruled by the V. O. C. Company officials refused to believe that the *Eendracht* had found a passage farther south than the Strait of Magellan. Accused of illegal trading, Le Maire and Schouten were sent back to Holland as prisoners. Jakob Le Maire died en route. His father, Isaac, later won a lawsuit against the V. O. C. and recovered his profits from the expedition.

EXPLORATION OF NEW HOLLAND, VAN DIEMEN'S LAND, AND NEW ZEALAND

The Dutch East India Company had developed a more or less official eastern route to Java and the Spice Islands by this time. Instead of sailing north from the Cape of Good Hope through the Indian Ocean, its ships were directed to take a more southern course west to take advantage of the prevailing winds. As Schouten and Le Maire were loading cloves onto their ship in Ternate, another *Eendracht,* this one captained by Dirk Hartog, was blown too far east on the company-approved route. Hartog turned his *Eendracht* north and spotted an island. Thinking it would be a good resting spot for the ship

en route to Java, he stopped and marked his discovery with a pewter plate. Hartog discovered an enormous landmass on the starboard (right) side of the ship as the *Eendracht* sped north to meet its appointed arrival time in Batavia. A conscientious servant of the V. O. C., Hartog did not make a landing but named it Eendrachtsland. When he reported his finding to the company, officials thought Eendrachtsland might be close to or part of the land Willem Janz had found, a vast expanse that had become known as New Holland.

The V. O. C. was inclined to finance further exploration of New Holland but was prevented because its ships and men were needed to stem English efforts to gain a footing in the East Indies. The English East India Company, established in 1600 by a group of London merchants, had sent only eight ships into the Indian Ocean by 1611, but the Dutch considered it a potentially dangerous rival. Not until the 1630s, when the English began to limit their trading to India, did the Dutch once more consider the question of New Holland. Little by little, though, the Dutch had learned more about its contours. Jan Carstenz, the first to chart Cape York and the Gulf of Carpenteria, sailed along its northern coast in 1622. He reported that the land was worthless to the Dutch and its people, "the poorest creatures I have ever seen."

The 1630s saw the height of Dutch global power. Ships from the Netherlands defeated Spanish forces in Chile, Peru, and Puerto Rico. The Dutch established a colony in North America at New Amsterdam. The Dutch West India Company, formed in 1621, carried out a bustling trade in the Caribbean. The Netherlands at last focused on acquiring the Great Southern Continent. Anthony Van Diemen became director-general of the Dutch East India Company in 1636. Van Diemen was determined to find out if New Holland was Terra Australis Incognita. In 1642 he engaged

Abel Janzoon Tasman to undertake an expedition to New Holland. The V. O. C. supplied two ships, the *Heemskirck* and the *Zeehaen*. Van Diemen gave Tasman explicit guidelines for the expedition. The men of the expedition should cause no harm to any native people they met. Tasman was to explain that the Dutch were not interested in conquering them, only in trading with them. The ships were provisioned with tantalizing samples of trade goods. The Dutch should pretend not to be interested in any gold, silver, or gems they found in new lands, but they should become very excited at the sight of copper or lead. Finally, if any indigenous people expressed an interest, they should be invited to return to Java with the expedition.

Van Diemen also dictated the route that Tasman should follow. Influenced by theories that Dutch navigator Frans Visscher had published in his *Memoir Concerning the Discovery of the Southland,* Van Diemen ordered Tasman first to sail *west,* to the island of Mauritius in the Indian Ocean. There, Tasman should replenish his supplies before sailing south to 54° latitude, and then east as far into the

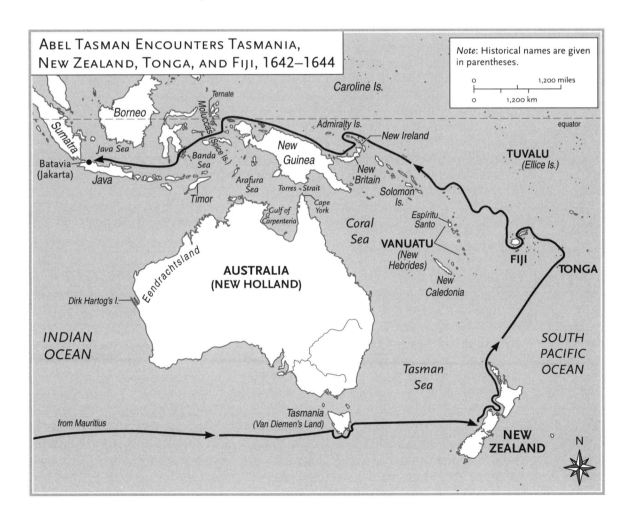

The Painted Prince

PACIFIC TRAVELERS IN EUROPE

Europeans had strange notions about the inhabitants of the lands their ships explored. Because the native peoples of the Pacific were not Christians, they were considered to be savages. Because some cultures practiced ritual cannibalism during wartime, Europeans believed all were man-eaters. In 18th-century romanticism, an idealization of nature influenced European art, literature, and philosophy. Native peoples were seen as "naturally" good, living life in a tropical Garden of Eden.

William Dampier bought a slave in Malaya to be his servant. When Dampier returned to England in 1691 he brought the heavily tattooed Malayan with him. Dampier, who came back almost penniless, exhibited the slave at London halls and at country fairs as "The Painted Prince." Like all Malayans, Dampier's slave had no immunity to European diseases. The Painted Prince died of smallpox after one year in England.

In 1768, as Bougainville's expedition prepared to leave Tahiti, an islander, Ahu-toru, asked to accompany the ships as a guide and interpreter. He also said that he wanted to see the Frenchman's country. The first native Pacific explorer of France arrived in Paris in March 1769. To the French, Ahu-Toru was the personification of the "noble savage" and he obliged the Parisians by posing for paintings wearing a luxurious version of "native" robes. The philosopher Denis Diderot argued that contact with Europeans ruined the "innocent and fortunate Tahitians." In a public letter to Bougainville, Diderot pleaded to him to "steer your vessel far, far away from their shores."

When Tobias Furneaux, commander of the *Adventure* on Cook's second voyage, brought Omai, a native of Huahine in the Society Islands, to England

Pacific Ocean as he could. This way, if the Great Southern Continent existed below the Tropic of Capricorn, Tasman would find it. Tasman arrived in Mauritius in early September 1642 and left a month later to sail farther south than had ever been attempted.

As the *Heemskirck* and the *Zeehaen* sailed south to the high latitudes, their sailors were exposed to intense cold and thick fog. They began to see icebergs, some as big as 10 miles long. At 49° south latitude Tasman decided that to proceed any farther south would risk losing ships and lives. Sailing north to the rel-

atively warmer waters and winds at 44° south latitude, the expedition traveled 4,000 miles to the east. The ships sailed right under New Holland without seeing it. Ship's surgeon Hendrik Haalbos wrote in his journal, "Discovered on 25 November a barren coast against which the sea beat boisterously." Tasman's log recorded that he sent the ship's carpenter to shore who "set up the flag of the House of Orange, tying it to a stake in which was cut the mark of the East India Company . . . the whole coast we named Antonius Van Diemen in honor of the Governor-General of our Com-in 1774, Omai was an overnight celebrity. He was presented to King George III, sketched by Sir Joshua Reynolds, and celebrated in poems. He inspired a craze for tattoos among English nobles. He was examined by scientists, inoculated against smallpox, and preached to by ministers hoping to convert him to Christianity. Daniel Solander, the naturalist who sailed on the *Endeavour*, wrote, "He is remarkably well behaved, easy in his manners, and remarkably complaisant to the Ladies."

In 1776, during James Cook's last voyage, Omai returned to Huahine. He was provided with a house, pots and pans, a small organ, a musket, a horse, and a globe of the world. Ten years later Omai's adventure was still famous. A popular comedy, *OMAI: Or, A Trip Around the World*, entertained thousands at London's Theater Royal.

Omai, a native of Huahine in the Society Islands, was famous in Europe, where he stayed for two years before returning home. *(National Archives of Canada)*

pany." The island found that day is now called Tasmania.

Tasman's ships did not linger at Van Diemen's Land but sailed to the northeast in search of the Solomons. When a lookout sighted land on December 13, Tasman thought they had arrived at Mendaña's islands. But Tasman had never read anything about high mountain peaks or dense forests of hardwoods in reports of Mendaña's voyages. Tasman had come to the west coast of New Zealand's South Island. As small boats from the *Heemskirck* and the *Zeehaen* explored a

lovely bay, Maori warriors in broad canoes attacked the shore party and killed three sailors. Haalbos reported Tasman's reaction, "noting that he could do nothing more except risk his men's lives against these savage people, named the place Murderers Bay and set sail."

As Tasman sailed north, the land seemed to go on forever, confirming his belief that he had at last found Terra Australis Incognita. His ships explored part of a great bay, but Tasman was unwilling to risk extensive reconnaissance. This bay was actually the strait between

New Zealand's two islands. Had Tasman chosen to investigate it, he would have realized that he would have to search elsewhere for the great southland. When Tasman reached the tip of New Zealand's North Island in February 1643, he directed the expedition east, into the open ocean. Having discovered that New Zealand was not the Solomons, Tasman thought he was bound to discover the islands that seemed to have been lost to Europeans for almost 50 years. His search was unsuccessful, but the *Heemskirck* and the *Zeehaen* did stop in Tonga, where Tasman noted of the Tongans, "Truly, they are a good and peaceful people, but excessively lascivious and wanton." Tasman's sailors were the first Europeans to see Fiji. Sailing proved to be dangerous in this reef-strewn part of the Pacific, and in March Tasman declined to push his luck by searching any longer for the Solomons.

Following the northern coast of New Guinea, Tasman's ships arrived in Batavia on June 15, 1643. The governor-general and the officials of the V. O. C. gave Tasman a cool reception. To their minds, he had failed in every aspect of his mission. Because he made no attempt to circumnavigate New Zealand, they had no idea if the coast he had found was really the western shore of Terra Australis Incognita. On his return voyage he had missed an opportunity to explore the southern coast of New Guinea and to determine if a passable strait existed between that island and New Holland. Most dismaying to the governor-general, Tasman had not found a single trading prospect.

THE LAST DUTCH EXPEDITION

Beginning in the 1650s, Dutch fortunes faded. The East India Company's success had glutted the European market for spice, and the taste for sugar from the Americas was growing in northern Europe. The Netherlands found itself at war with England between 1652 and 1654 and suffered defeat. While the Dutch did ultimately take Malacca from Spain and establish themselves at the Cape of Good Hope, the English were quickly surpassing them in shipbuilding and navigational science. When England and the Netherlands went to war again in 1664, the Netherlands lost its North American possessions. France now threatened the Netherlands as well. King Louis XIV, supported by England, invaded the Netherlands in 1672. The Glorious Revolution brought Holland's prince, William of Orange, to the throne of England in 1688. But even as the balance of power in Europe shifted, joining England and Holland together in challenging France, almost constant war had strained Holland's economy and forced it to acquire a substantial national debt.

In 1699 an earthquake and volcanic eruption destroyed the headquarters of the Dutch East India Company in Batavia, and annual epidemics of fever began to plague its remaining residents. The V. O. C. could no longer support exploration, and the Netherlands declined to underwrite any further expeditions to New Holland or to undertake any colonization efforts. In one last, late effort to stem the global decline of the Netherlands, the Dutch West India Company sent Jacob Roggeveen to find Terra Australis Incognita in 1721. Having read the records of Tasman's voyage, Roggeveen decided to travel south of the Tropic of Capricorn as well. His expedition, however, would approach the Great Southern Continent from the west. Roggeveen had read accounts of a large body of land southwest of Chile sighted by the English pirate Edward Davis in 1685. As with many who had read of it, Roggeveen thought this "Davisland" might be the southern continent.

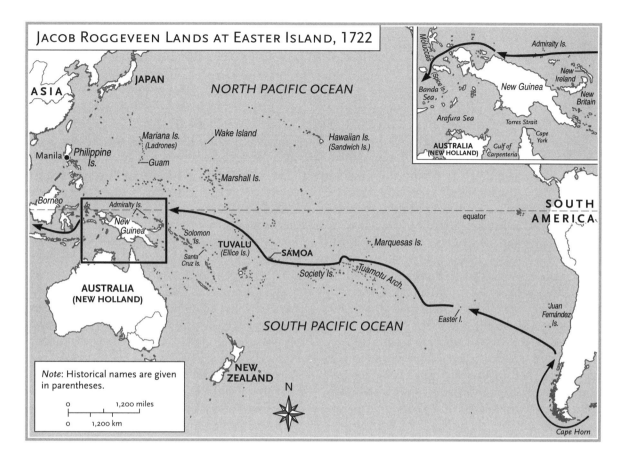

JACOB ROGGEVEEN LANDS AT EASTER ISLAND, 1722

Note: Historical names are given in parentheses.

Roggeveen's fleet of three ships—the *Arend,* the *Thienhoven,* and the *Africaanische Galey*—sailed through the Le Maire Strait around Cape Horn and continued, probably not intentionally, as far south as 62° south latitude. When Roggeveen spied huge icebergs, he was convinced they had been formed on the southern continent, but he found no land before the cold became intolerable to his crew and the ice threatened to crush his ships. Roggeveen sailed north into the warmth of the Pacific. His ships paused at Juan Fernandez, just off the Chilean coast, sailed southeast, and on Easter Sunday, April 5, 1722, anchored off an island that had not yet been recorded on a European map. Although the island, which Roggeveen named Easter, was small and not very fertile, the people there seemed friendly and Roggeveen's sailors were happy to go ashore to trade for provisions. The Dutch marveled at the huge stone heads, 30 feet high, that the islanders had constructed and that faced inland and ringed the island. Carl Behrens, an officer, speculated about the culture of the islanders in his journal, "The people appear to carry no weapons, but to rely on their gods or idols, great numbers of which had been erected on the beach."

By this time, having sailed farther south than even Tasman had attempted, Roggeveen was convinced that the Great Southern Continent did not exist anywhere near South America. If the continent did exist, its position was far, to the south and west. Even though his crew had acquired fresh food on Easter Island, many showed signs of scurvy, and all showed signs of exhaustion. Roggeveen decided to stop exploring and to sail into the charted water to the north. The expedition reached the Tuamotus group in May. The *Africaanische Galey* was wrecked on a reef by the island of Takaroa, and the other two ships took on the survivors. A supply party went ashore to fill water jars. Islanders attacked and killed 10 men. For almost two centuries European ships sailing west in the Pacific had stopped in the Tuamotus, and perhaps the islanders had come to expect violence and ill treatment.

Without replenishing water supplies and obtaining food in the Tuamotus, Roggeveen's ships were in deep trouble. As hard and fast as Roggeveen could force his ships to sail, he headed for the Dutch ports of the East Indies. Weeks passed, no islands were found, and men began to die. Carl Behrens used his expedition journals to write a memoir of the voyage. He vividly described the horror of the

summer months: "No pen can describe the misery of life on our ships. Only God knows what we have suffered. The ships reeked of death and the sick, and the stench alone was enough to make you ill." With scurvy bloating his men, covering them with open sores, and corpses thrown overboard most days, it seems inexplicable that Roggeveen passed the Society Islands and Samoa without stopping to take on water and food. His men may have been the first Europeans to see these lush islands, but it would remain for others to walk on their beaches.

After a year at sea Roggeveen's ships entered the now ruined and fever-infested port of Batavia. The officials of the Dutch East India Company considered Roggeveen no better than a pirate. Despite his commission from the Dutch West India Company, Roggeveen had assaulted the last shred of V. O. C. authority by sailing into the Pacific without a license. Company officials seized his ragged ships and sent Roggeveen and his officers to Holland as prisoners. The V. O. C. confiscated documents recording the voyage and findings of the Roggeveen expedition, telling its commander that the records were worthless. It was a sad conclusion to a great voyage, and a pitiful end for the age of Dutch voyages of exploration.

7

EXPLORATION IN THE SERVICE OF EMPIRE

Exploration in the Pacific Ocean during the 18th century, as in previous centuries, was shaped by events in Europe. When Spain's King Charles II died in 1700 he left his throne to Philip of Anjou, the grandson of France's Louis XIV. France had created a vast empire that included territories in Africa, India, and Canada and Louisiana in North America. The other nations of Europe feared the consequences if the New World possessions of France and Spain came under the same administration. In 1701 war broke out. France and Spain confronted the combined forces of England, Holland, Denmark, Austria, and Prussia. The War of the Spanish Succession consumed the treasuries, armies, and navies of the warring nations for 13 years and was carried to their territories overseas. British privateers captured or sank countless Spanish ships along the Pacific coast of South America.

When the Treaty of Utrecht brought an end to the war in 1714, few nations in Europe remained unchanged. Philip of Anjou was permitted to assume the Spanish throne but only on condition that Spain and France remain separate nations. Spain was entirely eclipsed as a world power and the Dutch star had set long before. France's treasury was almost empty, its armies disgraced, and its navy decimated. Louis XIV died in 1715, and the young Louis XV assumed the throne. His great task as an adult would be to rebuild France's might. After the 1707 Act of Union merged Scotland and England, Queen Anne ruled the United Kingdom of Great Britain. Anne died childless in 1714, and the British Parliament invited a German prince from Hanover to take the throne of the United Kingdom. The Parliament actually had greater power than the king, and the interests of Britain's merchants and traders dictated public and foreign policy. To increase trade, Parliament demanded that Spain grant the *asiento,* an exclusive right to trade with Spanish colonies that had been held by France, to Great Britain. British merchants grew rich from importing Spanish goods from America into Europe, and from the slave trade that was mandated by the asiento.

PIRATES POPULARIZE THE PACIFIC

By the 18th century Great Britain's commercial ships dominated trade across the Atlantic and in the Indian Ocean. Interest in the Pacific heightened as British merchant ships reported great opportunities for trading in China and the Indies created by the decline of Spanish and Dutch interests in the region. Reports of prospective wealth in the Pacific came from less respectable sources as well. Until the 18th century most of the Englishmen sailing in Pacific waters had been privateers or buccaneers, or gentleman pirates.

When buccaneer William Dampier published *A New Voyage Around the World* in 1692, he reported in a lively fashion his adventures in the Pacific in the 1680s. Under the renowned pirate Charles Swan on the *Cygnet,* Dampier had sailed up and down the western coasts of South and North America, capturing Spanish treasure ships from the Philippines. When Swan was deposed by his crew on nearby Guam—the ship had run so low on provisions that the crew proposed to kill and eat the officers—Dampier assumed command and sailed the *Cygnet* to the Philippines, China, and the Spice Islands. In 1688, Dampier reached New Holland. Dampier wrote in *A Voyage Around the World,* "It is not yet determined whether it is an island or a main continent, but I am certain it joins neither to Asia, Africa, nor America." He argued that while New Holland might not be the Great Southern Continent—he thought it barren and not worth further investigation—he was sure Terra Australis Incognita was located in the South Seas and urged England to make efforts to find it first.

Made more or less respectable by the popularity of his book, Dampier was offered command of the *Roebuck* in 1698 and directed by the British Admiralty to search for the southern continent. His orders were to sail around Cape Horn to 27° 20' south latitude, 400 miles west of Chile, and to confirm the existence of Davisland. He was then to proceed to New Holland, explore its as yet unseen eastern coastline, sail north to New Guinea, and then sail east looking for the continent. Because the *Roebuck* did not leave England until January 1699, and because the ship was already weather-beaten and creaking, Dampier decided not to risk a winter voyage around Cape Horn. He sailed for the Cape of Good Hope, making a wide detour to rid himself of his mutinous first lieutenant, George Fisher, in Brazil. Reaching New Holland on the last day of July, Dampier sailed north, charting the features of the dusty coast he named Dampierland.

With little water available on the shore, Dampier's crew began to suffer extreme thirst, while widespread scurvy further weakened them. Dampier brought the *Roebuck* to Timor, where he knew from his buccaneering days the Dutch had an armed base. From Timor, with the *Roebuck* repaired and its sailors rested and healthy, Dampier sailed to New Guinea. As he sailed east along New Guinea's northern coast, Dampier came to a very large, uncharted island that he named New Britain. Even though the *Roebuck* had been overhauled in Timor, it was leaking and on the point of foundering. Dampier's men were on the point of mutiny and forced him to take the ship back to Timor. In barely seaworthy condition after additional repairs, the *Roebuck* would never withstand the long voyage planned in search of the southern continent. Regretfully, Dampier set out across the Indian Ocean for the Cape of Good Hope and home.

In February 1701, having made the passage around the Cape, the *Roebuck* disintegrated, and its crew was shipwrecked on Ascension Island in the South Atlantic. Rescued by a trading ship, Dampier returned to England to find himself brought before a court-martial on charges stemming from his marooning George Fisher on the outbound journey. Dampier was found guilty and fined his entire pay for the voyage. Dampier realized his pen was his fortune and wrote the widely successful *Voyage to New Holland,* which not only got him out of debt but also aroused Britain's curiosity about New Holland and about the southern continent. Dampier made

two more voyages to the Pacific as a privateer during the War of the Spanish Succession. From 1702 to 1707 he captained the *St. George.* Between 1708 and 1711 he served with Woodes Rogers as pilot of the *Duke* and completed his third circumnavigation.

THE RISE OF BRITISH NAVAL POWER

While William Dampier's books sold thousands of copies, even more popular was Jonathan Swift's 1726 parody of his voyages,

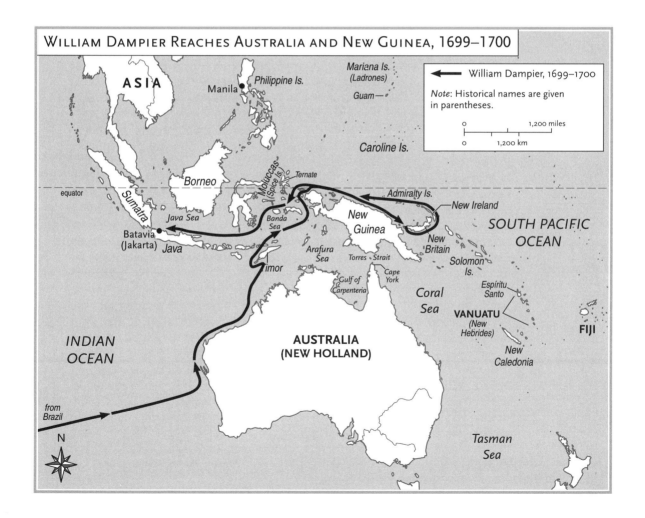

WILLIAM DAMPIER REACHES AUSTRALIA AND NEW GUINEA, 1699–1700

← William Dampier, 1699–1700

Note: Historical names are given in parentheses.

Gulliver's Travels. Daniel Defoe's *Robinson Crusoe* capitalized on the growing interest of the English reading public in books about the Pacific. When South Seas Company, founded to conduct trade between Great Britain and South America and the islands of the South Pacific, offered its stocks for sale in 1720, thousands of investors, dreaming of islands and of profits, rushed to purchase shares. While British merchant ships made fortunes for private companies and individuals, the British government, led by Robert Walpole, seemed uninterested in deploying its ships to the Pacific. When William Pitt, whose family had achieved great wealth in the India trade, was elected to Parliament in 1735, he

The Real Robinson Crusoe

In April 1719, Daniel Defoe published *The Life and Strange Surprizing Adventures of Robinson Crusoe, of York, Mariner: Who lived Eight and Twenty Years, all alone in an uninhabited Island on the Coast of America, near the Mouth of the Great River of Oroonoque; Having been cast on Shore by Shipwreck, wherein all the Men perished but himself. With An Account how he was at last as strangely deliver'd by Pyrates.* The book, with its two sequels, became known simply as *Robinson Crusoe* and is considered to be the first novel in the English language. It is also the most widely read book in history, other than the Bible. By the end of the 19th century more than 700 editions, adaptations, and translations of this famous story had filled bookshelves all over the world.

In 1704, Alexander Selkirk, the historical inspiration for Crusoe, was second-in-command on the *Cinque Ports,* a privateer searching for Spanish treasure ships in the Pacific. The captain of the *Cinque Ports,* Thomas Stradling, was a violent man and a poor leader. Supplies on the ship were running low, no Spanish ships had been sighted, and the crew was on the verge of mutiny. Moreover, Selkirk felt the *Cinque Ports* was not seaworthy. Selkirk asked to be put ashore on Juan Fernandez, an island off the coast of Chile. First explored in 1574, Juan Fernandez had a good supply of wood, fresh water, and wild goats. Its sheltered bay frequently harbored French and English ships before they set off into the Pacific. Selkirk figured that other crew members, convinced of the poor prospects of the *Cinque Ports,* would join him, and that they would wait no more than three or four months to be rescued.

None of his shipmates volunteered to leave the ship, and Selkirk was set ashore with his sea chest, a Bible, a cooking pot, a musket, charts and maps, some tobacco, a cask of rum, and a day's worth of cheese and jam. Selkirk would live alone on Juan Fernandez more than four years. He built two huts for shelter, used goatskins to make clothing, and nourished himself on fish, seals, lobsters, goat, and vegetables planted years before by Spanish sailors. With no one to talk to, Selkirk lost his ability to speak. Irritated by raiding rats at night, challenged Walpole to expand Britain's empire.

Spain, though it honored Great Britain's rights under the asiento, was irritated by the activities of British smugglers in the Caribbean and Pacific. When Spain began to seize illegal cargoes and to board British merchant ships to inspect them, British merchants lobbied Parliament to protect free trade and to use Britain's navy to guarantee the freedom of the seas. Pitt, arguing that Spain's recent alliance with an increasingly powerful France would threaten Great Britain, resuscitated an incident from 1731 in which Spanish coast guards had mutilated an English merchant sailor. Holding a severed

Selkirk lured wild cats into his hut with goat meat and sometimes had more than 100 cats as company. Most nights he lit a bonfire on a hill, hoping to signal a passing ship.

In early 1709, Selkirk spied sails on the horizon. As the ship came closer to Juan Fernandez, he recognized the English flag and ran to meet the rowboats sent from the *Duke,* captained by privateer Woodes Rogers. At the time of the rescue, Rogers nicknamed Selkirk the "Governor of this Island, its *Absolute Monarch.*"

This Currier & Ives lithograph pictures the fictional Robinson Crusoe surrounded by many pets and a wrecked ship in the distance. *(Library of Congress, Prints and Photographs Division [LC-USZ62-25213])*

In this Currier & Ives lithograph, Robinson Crusoe and companion Friday carry guns while walking through lush vegetation. *(Library of Congress, Prints and Photographs Division [LC-USZC2-2963])*

ear preserved in a jar of alcohol as he addressed Parliament, Pitt pressed Great Britain to put an end to the last sputter of Spanish might.

In 1739, Great Britain declared war on Spain. The War of Jenkins' Ear carried Britain's navy into the Pacific. George Anson was sent with six warships and nearly 1,000 men to capture and destroy Spanish ships off South America. Twenty years of peace had rendered the Royal Navy a bureaucratic mess of corruption. It was barely able to enlist, bribe, and kidnap enough men to send with Anson's

fleet. Once on the ships, sailors faced inhuman conditions. Overcrowded and poorly ventilated, an English man-o-war offered ideal conditions for the spread of disease. Dishonest suppliers would sell the navy meat that was already rotting in its cask and biscuits made from flour mixed with sawdust. Crews were comprised of merchant sailors drugged and kidnapped by press gangs in harbor towns, convicts released to the authority of enlistment officers, and men who had no better option. Faced with frequent insubordination and the threat of mutiny, officers sometimes resorted to outright torture in maintaining discipline.

Anson's fleet set sail for the Pacific in September 1740 beset with barely seaworthy ships, crews of resentful and inexperienced sailors, and provisions Anson knew to be insufficient. Men began to die even before the fleet reached Cape Horn. Four ships were lost by the time the fleet reached Juan Fernandez, where Anson intended to establish a base for further forays into the Pacific. Achieving moderate success in capturing Spanish ships in the waters around Juan Fernandez, Anson

To support Great Britain during the War of Jenkins' Ear, George Anson fought Spanish forces, capturing their ships off the coast of South America. *(Library of Congress, Prints and Photographs Division [LC-USZ62-122002])*

decided to pursue the greatest prize, the annual Galleon from Manila. Failing to intercept the Galleon off Acapulco, Anson scuttled all but his two largest ships, the *Gloucester* and the *Centurion,* and set off for the Philippines in late March 1742.

In all the difficult crossings of the Pacific, the Anson expedition stands out as particularly horrible. The normal northeasterly trade winds failed. After seven weeks of sailing, the fleet was a quarter of the way to the Philippines. The ships were rotting, and the *Gloucester's* mainmast had to be cut down. The *Centurion* was leaking so badly that its crew manned pumps day and night to keep it afloat. Of the 77 men on the *Gloucester,* more than 50 were too ill with scurvy to work. On August 16, in open ocean, Anson was forced to scuttle the *Gloucester* and take its men and equipment on board the *Centurion.* Grateful to reach Tinian, a small island in the Marianas group, 10 days later, Anson anchored the *Centurion* and sent most of the crew ashore to recover from their ordeal. A violent storm arose one night and Anson woke to find the *Centurion* gone. The lines securing its anchor had rotted, and the ship and its skeleton crew were blown out to sea.

Nineteen days later, when Anson had almost given up hope, the *Centurion* reappeared. Anson knew his ship was in no condition to take on the Spanish gunships of Manila. He sailed to China, where the English East India Company had a post in Canton. Over the next six months the *Centurion* was refitted and made seaworthy. Anson told officials and his own men that the *Centurion* was heading for England when it left the harbor at Canton in April 1743. Instead, the ship sailed to the Philippines and successfully attacked the annual Galleon in June. Anson captured the *Nuestra Señora de Covadonga.* When the *Centurion* sailed into port a year later, Anson

The South Seas Bubble

The South Seas Company was formed in 1711 under the leadership of Robert Harley. In a complex transaction, £9 million worth of government bonds was exchanged for stock in the new company. Investors believed that the South Seas Company would be granted a monopoly on the South Seas trade and were attracted by the company's excellent 6 percent dividend. Without ever carrying out much trade, the company saw its worth increase dramatically. By 1720, after bribing many government officials and members of the court of King George I, the South Seas Company proposed to assume the national debt of Great Britain and issued more stock. Stock prices soared. In January 1720 the price of a share was £182. By August the same share sold for £1,000. Jonathan Swift, the author of *Gulliver's Travels,* wrote a friend, "I have enquired of some that have come from London, what is the religion there? They tell me it is South Sea stock."

Such high prices attracted speculators who sought to drive up the price of the stock and sell their shares at great profit. High prices also attracted fraudulent schemes and unwise investors. In September 1720 the price of the stock— in no way supported by the actual worth of the South Seas Company—crashed to £135. Banks failed. Mobs gathered in London as Parliament was recalled. Many people, including government ministers, lost their fortunes. Fraud was discovered to be rampant within the South Seas Company, but full investigation was prevented when company officials fled England, destroying or taking with them damning evidence. The South Seas Bubble, with its deluded investors inspired by the promise of fabulous wealth in the South Pacific, was the first financial scandal in modern history. The physicist Isaac Newton, who lost

was a hero. He had seized from Spain more than a million gold pieces and 35,000 ounces of silver. In 1751, Anson was made First Lord of the Admiralty and became a powerful force for reform of the Royal Navy.

FRANCE AND GREAT BRITAIN RACE TO TERRA AUSTRALIS INCOGNITA

Anson's victory in the Pacific increased British interest in further exploration. In 1744, John Campbell published a new edition of John Harris's 1705 *Book of Voyages.* In his introduc-

tion Campbell argued that Great Britain should send its ships to find the Great Southern Continent. Such an endeavor, especially if successful, would "greatly increase our shipping and seamen, which are the true and natural strength of this country." Campbell further recommended that Britain annex the Falkland Islands in the Atlantic and Juan Fernandez in the Pacific and establish naval bases to support the search for Terra Australis Incognita. Campbell also became the first to suggest that Great Britain should colonize New Holland. Frenchman Charles de Brosses had the same thoughts, although of course he felt the Pacific should belong to France. He

£20,000 in the bubble, remarked, "I can calculate the motions of the heavenly bodies, but not the madness of people."

In 1720 the South Seas Company's stock soared. Here, stock traders crowd a village square in England. *(Library of Congress, Prints and Photographs Division [LC-USZ62-86728])*

published a history of Pacific exploration in 1756, in which he wrote that Quirós had discovered and landed on the southern continent. De Brosses appealed to the national pride of the French as his book urged an expedition. "The most celebrated of monarchs will be the one who gives his name to the Southern Land."

Both France and Great Britain accepted the challenge. Louis-Antoine de Bougainville volunteered to start a French colony in the Falkland Islands and brought 27 settlers to the islands in 1764. The colonists included French-speaking refugees from Acadia who had been cruelly displaced from their homes

in Canada after Great Britain won the Seven Years' War in 1763. Just as Bougainville's colonists were settling there, Britain sent John Byron to the Falklands.

Byron, nicknamed Foul Weather Jack by his sailors, had sailed with Anson as a midshipman, an officer in training. Byron's secret orders were ambitious. The Royal Navy ships the *Dolphin* and the *Tamar* were to sail under Byron's command to survey the Falklands for future use as a naval station. Byron was then to pass through the Strait of Magellan to the Pacific and up the coast of America. The British government was interested in northern California, claimed as New Albion by

Louis-Antoine de Bougainville founded a French colony on the Falkland Islands. *(Library of Congress, Prints and Photographs Division [LC-USZ62-86717])*

Francis Drake. More significantly, the Admiralty wanted Byron to search for a northwest passage. If no such passage to the Atlantic was found, Byron was directed to sail for the Cape of Good Hope while keeping a look out for the Great Southern Continent.

Arriving at the Falklands in June, but having no knowledge of Bougainville's colony, Byron claimed the islands for Great Britain. His ships entered the Strait of Magellan in February 1765 and, in an extraordinary coincidence, encountered Bougainville's ships there. Bougainville had gone to cut timber for his colony. The two captains ignored each other, but both sent reports of their rival's presence to Europe. Once through the strait, Byron disobeyed his orders to go to New Albion and to search for the Northwest Pas-

sage. Instead, the *Dolphin* and the *Tamar* would sail west to find the Solomons, unvisited since Mendaña's ships departed in 1595, and to search for the southern continent. By the time Byron returned to England in early May 1766, he had circumnavigated the globe. His expedition failed to find the Solomons, failed to find Terra Australis Incognita, and failed to discover any new lands.

Byron's lackluster voyage might have dampened British enthusiasm for another expedition. Within a year of Byron's return, however, the Admiralty refitted the *Dolphin* and sent it to the Pacific with a new captain, Samuel Wallis. Philip Carteret, who had served on the *Tamar*, was made captain of a companion ship, the *Swallow*. The Admiralty ordered the expedition to find the southern continent and claim possession for Great Britain. The ships were to sail as far west as 120° longitude and then return quickly to England by way of the Cape of Good Hope. The ships left Portsmouth on August 22, 1766.

The *Swallow* was a slow, awkward, aging ship. The Admiralty had promised Carteret that a modern frigate would be waiting in the Falklands to replace the *Swallow*. The expedition reached the Falklands in November, but no substitute frigate arrived. The *Swallow* would have to make the voyage. From January through April 1767 the ships struggled through the Strait of Magellan. The *Dolphin* entered the Pacific well ahead of the *Swallow*. Wallis took advantage of a temperamental wind and began to advance into the open ocean. When the *Swallow* emerged from the strait, battered and leaking, there was no sign of the *Dolphin*. The two captains had failed to designate a rendezvous and, after a brief search for the *Dolphin*, Carteret decided to sail across the Pacific and back to England.

Carteret's voyage rivals Anson's as a tale of misery. When the *Swallow* reached Juan Fer-

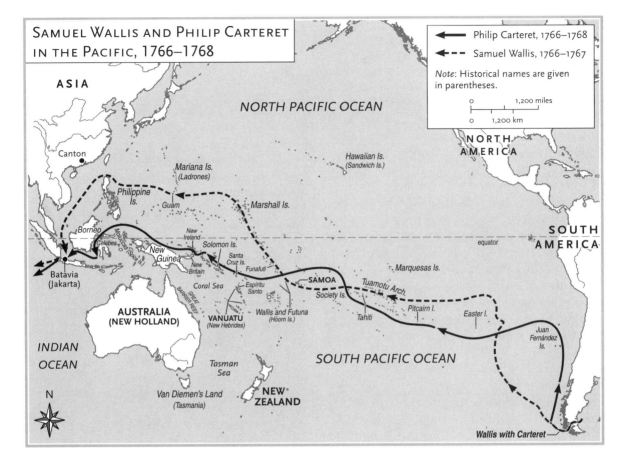

SAMUEL WALLIS AND PHILIP CARTERET
IN THE PACIFIC, 1766–1768

→ Philip Carteret, 1766–1768
→--- Samuel Wallis, 1766–1767

Note: Historical names are given in parentheses.

0   1,200 miles
0   1,200 km

ASIA

NORTH PACIFIC OCEAN

NORTH AMERICA

Canton

Mariana Is.
(Ladrones)

Hawaiian Is.
(Sandwich Is.)

Philippine Is.

Guam

Marshall Is.

Borneo

New Ireland

Celebes

Moluccas (Spice Is.)

New Guinea

Solomon Is.

Santa Cruz Is.

Funafuti

equator

SOUTH AMERICA

Batavia
(Jakarta)

New Britain

Espíritu Santo

Coral Sea

SAMOA

Marquesas Is.

Society Is.

Tuamotu Arch.

Pitcairn I.

Easter I.

Juan Fernández Is.

VANUATU
(New Hebrides)

Wallis and Futuna
(Hoorn Is.)

Tahiti

GREAT BARRIER REEF

INDIAN OCEAN

AUSTRALIA
(NEW HOLLAND)

Tasman Sea

SOUTH PACIFIC OCEAN

N

Van Diemen's Land
(Tasmania)

NEW ZEALAND

Wallis with Carteret

nández, in desperate need of repair, hostile Spanish forces occupied the island. The next land that was sighted was a tiny island with a shore so rocky there was no place to land. Carteret named the island Pitcairn, after the crewmember who first saw it. The *Swallow* slowly sailed west, its crew pumping constantly to compensate for leaks in the hull. As scurvy developed, men became too weak to work. Only coral islands devoid of water and vegetation appeared. After four months in the Pacific, the *Swallow* approached a group of large islands on August 12. Carteret named them the Queen Charlotte Islands. Mendaña and Quirós had known them as the Santa Cruz

group. A party was sent ashore to get much-needed food and water. When some islanders, perhaps more curious than hostile, crowded the landing boat, Carteret's men fired their guns. Several crewmembers were killed, and Carteret sped the *Swallow* away from the island.

Sailing west, the *Swallow* was prevented from seeking shelter at another group of large islands when warriors in canoes prevented Carteret from even lowering a landing boat from his ship. Carteret did not realize that he had found the Solomons at last. He may not have cared by this time. His men were dying from scurvy. His ship was leaking and covered in barnacles. Its sails were in rags and its lines were rotting. Once more, the *Swallow* set sail in search of a safe anchorage. On August 26, Carteret arrived at the island William Dampier had called New Britain. The *Swallow* anchored in the long inlet named St. George's Bay by Dampier. Finally, Carteret's men were able to eat and drink. Carteret did enough exploring to find that St. George's Bay was a strait separating New Britain from a large island Carteret named New Ireland.

Carteret realized that he had to get the *Swallow* and his sailors to a port where the ship could be overhauled and his men cared for. The closest port was in the Dutch East Indies, a thousand miles away. Not until December did the *Swallow* arrive at the island of Celebes. As it crept along the northern coast of New Guinea, monsoon winds had blown the *Swallow* back to the Philippines. Half of Carteret's men had died. Many of the survivors were sick with malaria. Dutch officials at Celebes refused to help, offering aid only after Carteret literally begged them to. When his men were well and the most pressing leaks in his ship fixed, Carteret took the *Swallow* to Batavia for major repairs. In March 1769 the *Swallow* sailed up the Thames. Wallis and the *Dolphin* had returned almost a year before with a very different tale of the Pacific.

As the *Swallow*'s voyage had been hellish, the *Dolphin*'s was heavenly. Although strong winds had prevented Wallis from sailing to 120° west longitude, and the *Dolphin* had traveled two months seeing no islands until the Tuamotu group, in late June its lookout spied a large island on the horizon. Wallis was sure he had found the southern continent. When the *Dolphin* arrived at the island on June 23, 1767, it was clear it was too small to be Terra Australis Incognita. The British were struck by the island's beauty and eager to land. Anchoring close to the shore in a broad, calm

bay, the *Dolphin* was immediately attacked by islanders throwing rocks. Wallis ordered his gunners to fire the ship's cannons to drive the people inland. Waiting three days to be sure the islanders were gone from the beach, Wallis went ashore and claimed the island for Great Britain, naming it King George III Island.

The islanders slowly returned to their houses and began to bring food and water to the British sailors. Wallis ordered his men to treat the people kindly and to avoid any violence. As the days passed, communication improved. The British sailors exchanged trade

John Byron encountered de Bougainville's ships in the Strait of Magellan. In this illustration, Byron greets some inhabitants of Patagonia. *(Library of Congress, Prints and Photographs Division [LC-USZ62-70701])*

goods for pigs, chickens, and fruit. Wallis understood from them that the island was named Otaheite. Tahiti, as the British referred to it, seemed like the Garden of Eden. Its people were as beautiful as its flowers and beaches. Tahitian women, who found no shame in open sexuality, entranced Wallis's sailors. After a month spent exploring Tahiti and neighboring islands, the British were very sorry to leave. As a gesture of affection, and perhaps to provide for future British ships, Wallis planted peach, plum, and cherry trees before the *Dolphin* sailed on July 27. When

Wallis arrived in England in May 1768, he reported that he had not found the southern continent, but he had found paradise.

Antoine Bougainville had hurried back to France after he passed John Byron's ship in the Strait of Magellan in 1765. Within a year he had gained a commission to go to the Pacific. The French government ordered him to find the southern continent and to locate and claim an island that would allow French ships easy access to the trading centers of China. Philibert Commerson was enlisted to serve as the expedition's naturalist and to collect plant specimens and conduct experiments during the voyage. Commerson was the first of many scientists who would accompany voyages of exploration. On November 15, 1766, the frigate *Bodeuse* sailed from the French port of Nantes. Bougainville's first duty was to put in at the Falklands. France had agreed to quit its claims on the islands, and Bougainville was to facilitate the transfer of the islands to Spanish authorities.

Having accomplished the transfer, Bougainville arrived in Rio de Janeiro in June 1767 and rendezvoused with his cargo ship, the *Etoile*. Not until early December did Bougainville's ship enter the Strait of Magellan. Fighting high winds and bitter cold, the ships made a slow passage. This frustrated Bougainville all the more, because he was anxious to overtake Wallis and Carteret in the race to the southern continent. On January 26, 1768, the *Bodeuse* and the *Etoile* entered the Pacific. In early March, Bougainville reached the Tuamotu islands and then encountered heavy rains.

His lookouts could easily have missed seeing the peaks of an island on the horizon. As Bougainville's ships approached the island on April 6, they chose to anchor in a lagoon shadowed by a lushly forested peak. Bougainville recorded in his journal that on the shore stood "pretty, almost naked women." Bougainville landed and claimed the island for France. An act of possession was inscribed on a wooden plank and buried on the beach. Bougainville called the island New Cythera. The islanders told him they called it Otaheite. Bougainville saw signs that the British had preceded him. Some Tahitians wore articles of European clothing. Islanders had mirrors and metal utensils. If Bougainville was disappointed, he did not record it in his journal. He wrote, "I felt as though I had been transported to the Garden of Eden. Everywhere we found peace,

innocent joy, and every appearance of happiness. What a country! What a people!"

When the French ships left on April 15, a Tahitian man named Ahu-Toru went with them to serve as a guide. Rather than following the course of previous expeditions to New Guinea and then to the Moluccas, Bougainville began to search in earnest for Terra Australis Incognita. Within a few weeks his ships had passed through the Samoan islands and entered the New Hebrides. Some islands had people who welcomed the French ships. Many of the islands were inhospitable. Bougainville claimed all of them for France. Most of Bougainville's men were now suffering from scurvy, and some from a sexually transmitted disease Ahu-Toru called "the English disease."

When the *Bodeuse* and the *Etoile* left the New Hebrides, Bougainville recognized the island of Espíritu Santo from the records of Quirós's expedition. Bougainville decided to continue sailing west to resolve the question of whether Quirós had indeed touched up the shores of the Great Southern Continent. His ships entered the Coral Sea until they arrived at a wall of surf caused by an endless tangle of rocky low-lying islands, reefs, and sandbars. It was the Great Barrier Reef. Bougainville knew he could go no further west. Sailing north toward New Guinea, his ships began to run short of provisions. Hunger tormented the men to the point that they killed and ate a pet dog.

Bougainville would not risk his men by taking the time to confirm whether a strait existed between New Holland and New Guinea. He was concerned to get the Dutch posts in the Moluccas as soon as possible. Winds, tides, and hostile islanders prevented the *Bodeuse* and the *Etoile* from landing in the Solomons, islands that Bougainville did not recognize from his charts. West of the

Solomons the ships were able to anchor on July 6, 1768, at New Ireland. Bougainville's men joyfully went ashore to find food, but New Ireland offered little. Disappointed, the men returned to ships after finding the remnants of Carteret's camp. On August 11, Bougainville began his passage along New Guinea's northern coast. Men grew weaker every day from hunger and scurvy. At the end of the month the ships reached Ceram in the Moluccas and were able at last to take on food and water.

From Ceram, Bougainville sailed to Batavia. He learned that the *Swallow* had departed only 12 days earlier. Bougainville badly wanted to overtake the *Swallow,* and another fever epidemic gave him no reason to linger at Batavia. Leaving the *Etoile* to be repaired in Batavia, Bougainville raced across the Indian Ocean to the Cape of Good Hope. On January 9, 1769, an official at the Cape told him he was only three days behind Carteret. The two ships met on February 25. Looking at Carteret's ruined ship, Bougainville could not believe that the *Swallow* had survived the trip around the Cape of Good Hope, let alone years of hard sailing in the Pacific. Bougainville and Carteret exchanged greetings. Neither man, both now circumnavigators, discussed his voyage.

On March 16, Bougainville brought the *Bodeuse* into the harbor at Saint-Malo on the northern coast of France. He had sailed around the world. His men had suffered hunger and disease, but only nine had died. He brought with him Ahu-Toru, living proof of a tropical paradise. Bougainville gave French scientists hundreds of botanical specimens and drawings prepared by Philibert Commerson. Still, Bougainville's expedition, like those of Wallis and Carteret, had not found the southern continent.

The British press, members of Parliament, and the Royal Society, founded in 1660 "for the promoting of Physico-Mathematicall Experimentall Learning," called for a great expedition in search of the Great Southern Continent. In 1767, Alexander Dalrymple published *An Account of the Discoveries Made in the South Pacific Oceans Previous to 1764.* Dalrymple had returned to England from the East with the specific purpose of promoting exploration and trade in the Pacific. He added to his firsthand knowledge of the Pacific with intense study of all available records of Portuguese, Spanish, and Dutch expeditions to the Pacific. From these, he constructed a very detailed description of the southern land. He told his readers that the landmass would be found about 40° south latitude, that it was approximately 5,300 miles long, and that its population would number 50 million. Dalrymple convinced many that Britain's greatness depended on finding the southern continent before the French got there first. The race to Terra Australis Incognita was far from over.

8

JAMES COOK
AND THE *ENDEAVOUR*

 "October 27, 1728. James, Ye Son of a Day Labourer, James Cook, and of his wife, Grace." So reads the parish register in Marton, Yorkshire. Greatness was not the birthright of James Cook. Like most men in 18th-century Britain, Cook seemed destined to follow in the footsteps of his barely literate father and to make a meager living managing the holdings of a local landlord. Cook's first mentor, his father's employer, noticed the young boy's aptitude and paid his fees at the village school. Cook not only learned to read and write but displayed a surprising aptitude for mathematics. A world beyond rural, agricultural Yorkshire opened to Cook. At the age of 18 he left his family home and went to the port of Whitby, becoming an apprentice on the five-ton collier, or coal ship, *Freelove*.

Cook gave good service to his employers, the shipping firm Walkers. His uncommon sense for piloting cargo through the rough North Sea was accompanied by a reputation for honesty and regularity in carrying out orders. Walkers promoted him to mate at age 23, and Cook was positioned to be given command of a new ship the firm had commissioned. A successful career as a merchant ship's commander might well have been his, but Cook supposed that a greater future lay before him.

Great Britain's colonial possessions in North America provided needed revenue for the Crown and served as a bulwark of Britain's global power. By 1755 a war to gain France's Canadian territory seemed certain. Britain's naval superiority in the looming Seven Years' War was in no way assured. Even with the reforms begun by George Anson, First Lord of the Admiralty, sailors were often pressed into service, literally kidnapped from harborside taverns and London slums. Most British officers were younger sons of the aristocracy who chose naval careers out of duty or desperation and who rose in the ranks by family connections. Still, Cook saw the impending colonial conflict as his next opportunity. "I had a mind," he wrote, "to try my fortune that way."

John Webber painted this portrait of Captain James Cook at the Cape of Good Hope in 1776. *(National Archives of Canada)*

On June 17, 1755, he enlisted in the Royal Navy as a common able-bodied seaman.

Six feet tall, Cook had to crouch below decks of the *Eagle,* a 60-gun ship manned by 400 and commanded by Captain Sir Hugh Palliser. Cook's seagoing experience quickly became obvious and valuable. Within a month of joining the *Eagle,* Cook was made master's mate. Six months later in Canada, Palliser promoted him to the greater responsibilities of boatswain and rewarded Cook's considerable aptitude for navigation and mathematics with special training in surveying and cartography. Upon returning from successful action in Canada, Cook passed a written examination and attained the rank of ship's master in June 1757. He had risen from the lowest status in the Royal Navy to its highest noncommis-

sioned rank in two years. The Seven Years' War had indeed proved Cook's main chance for advancement, and it had provided him with another powerful mentor in Palliser.

Certainly Cook could expect no greater future than to be made ship's master—taking charge of navigation, of the piloting of a ship, and of the supervision of a crew. He was no gentleman, and he had no important connections. Yet, as master of the *Pembroke* and the *Northumberland,* Cook impressed his military and social superiors as he charted the St. Lawrence River, thus enabling the British to gain control of Quebec. "From my experience of Mr. Cook's genius and capacity, I think him well-qualified for the work he has performed and for greater undertakings of the same kind," wrote Lord Colville, captain of the *Northumberland.* Cook's mentor, Hugh Palliser, by 1764 governor of Newfoundland, arranged for Cook's next undertaking. Entitled "Mr. James Cook, Engineer" and "the King's Surveyor," Cook was given the command of the *Grenville* and distinguished himself by compiling charts of Newfoundland so accurate they were used well into the 20th century.

COOK IS OFFERED COMMAND OF THE *ENDEAVOUR*

Even in a career of opportunities grasped and influential men impressed, the chance offered to James Cook in 1768 stands out in sharp relief. Forty years old, Cook was a noncommissioned officer of obscure birth and rough breeding. Still, the most important assignment in the history of the Royal Navy was his. Having dispatched France's ambitions in North America, Britain was eager to thwart its claims to the Great Southern Continent. John Montagu, fourth earl of Sandwich and sometime First Lord of the Admiralty, was the genius of 18th-century British imperialism. Joseph Banks was a fantastically wealthy gentleman, a botanist, and a member of the Royal Society. Banks's driving ambition was to be an important figure in the scientific establishment. Montagu and Banks combined forces to persuade King George III to finance an expedition to the South Seas.

George III had incurred great debts in the war with France that lasted from 1756–63 and was troubled by rumors of rebellion in the 13 American colonies. The king was anxious to gain the support of the Royal Navy for any

Botanist Joseph Banks was one of many individuals with specialized knowledge to accompany James Cook's expedition aboard the *Endeavour. (Library of Congress, Prints and Photographs Division [LC-USZ62-120897])*

future wars and could do so by putting this important project under the command of the Admiralty. Montagu, alert to the possibilities of new colonial enterprises, favored camouflaging a voyage of territorial discovery in the guise of one of scientific exploration. Banks, a civilian, wanted command of the expedition so that he could satisfy his hunger for significant discovery without constraint. The solution crafted was to appoint a Royal Navy officer not so well connected or independent that he would question Banks's superiority but still capable and experienced in the seafaring sciences. Montagu consulted Cook's old supporter Hugh Palliser about an appropriate candidate. On May 25, 1768, Cook received his commission in the Royal Navy, with the rank of first lieutenant, and was named commander of the expedition.

Remembering the seaworthiness of the colliers he had piloted in the North Seas, Cook selected the HMS *Endeavour* to carry the expedition. The collier, about the size of four average suburban houses, was fitted to Cook's specifications and included a veritable floating laboratory with compact space for preparing and storing biological specimens. The *Endeavour* could carry 18 months of provisions and 94 men. Along with officers and sailors, the ship's company included botanist Joseph Banks, naturalist Daniel Solander, astronomer Charles Green, and artists Alexander Buchan and Sydney Parkinson.

The stated purpose for the voyage was to study the Transit of Venus, the crossing of that planet in front of the sun, to occur on June 3, 1769. This astronomical phenomenon would not occur again for a century, and precise observation and calculation would allow the measurement of the Earth's distance from the sun. Britain planned two observatories in the Northern Hemisphere and a third in the

Artists Aboard ⌒

All three of James Cook's Pacific expeditions included artists and draftsmen in their crews. Alexander Buchan and Sydney Parkinson sailed on the *Endeavour,* William Hodges on the first voyage of the *Resolution,* and John Webber on the *Resolution*'s second trip. In a time before photography, classically trained artists worked with expedition naturalists to record the plants and animals encountered in new lands. They added to geographic knowledge by depicting the features of coastlines in great detail. Hodges painted these coastal features by observation, through the large glass windows in Cook's cabin and by going ashore. This gave his work a level of accuracy that surpassed paintings created from sketches. Maritime artists made the only visual record of planetary patterns and climactic phenomena. Hodges became famous for the way he captured the unique qualities of Antarctic light.

The most important contribution of Cook's artists was their portrayal of the people encountered on the voyages. Parkinson's first anthropological studies were of the inhabitants of Tierra del Fuego. Hodges captured in detail the war canoes of the Tahitians and their crews. And Webber's drawings of the people of the Bering Strait, Aleutian Islands, and Alaskan coasts introduced these cultures to the Europeans.

South, in the Pacific. Samuel Wallis returned to England that same May and reported that Tahiti would be an ideal location. Scientific inquiry was simply one goal for *Endeavour*'s men. Unstated and unrevealed was the more important object: the discovery and possession of new territory for Great Britain. News of Louis-Antoine de Bougainville's landing on Tahiti heightened Britain's desire to consolidate claims on the islands of the South Seas. The expedition assumed a secretive urgency. The Admiralty delivered a second, sealed set of orders to Cook, to be opened only after the observation of the Transit of Venus. The officers were also required to agree to turn over the ship's logs and their own journals upon return to England. No member of the crew was to reveal the expedition's route without permission from the Admiralty.

THE *ENDEAVOUR* SETS SAIL

The *Endeavour* sailed from Plymouth on August 25, 1768. Cook's direct, deliberate, and confident manner supported his renowned skill and accomplishment. Much to the surprise and dismay of the aristocratic and snobbish Banks, James Cook was a singularly effective commander. Cook demanded from his crew an exacting code of behavior and strict hygiene. In sharp contrast to the squalor common in the Royal Navy, the *Endeavour* and its men were clean and healthy. A large store of vinegar was brought on board and used to disinfect the crew's quarters. Water barrels were emptied and scrubbed at each opportunity to refill them with fresh water. Cold baths were ordered whenever possible.

Scurvy
"THE SAILOR'S DISEASE"

Sixteenth-century English mariner Richard Hawkins called scurvy "the plague of the Sea, the spoyle of Mariners." He wrote, "in twentie years since I haue vsed the Sea, I take vpon me to giue accompt of ten thousand men consumed with the disease." Scurvy is a deficiency of vitamin C, which is abundant in fresh fruits and vegetables, especially in citrus fruits. Until the late 18th century, sailors' diets were limited to foods that could be stored on long voyages. Except for time spent in harbors and the first few days out of port, meals on ships consisted of dried or salted foods—meats and beans or peas—and biscuits made of wheat flour or other grains. After a month or so, sailors would report a feeling of weakness and pain in their muscles. As the disease progressed, men's teeth would become so loose they could pull them out with their hands. Internal bleeding and opening of old wounds would occur. Diarrhea, fever, kidney failure, and lung collapse would ultimately cause death. The expectation that large numbers of crew would perish from scurvy resulted in overcrowded ships. Captains wanted to ensure sufficient crew numbers, even if half their company died during a voyage. On many voyages, well more than half the crew perished. During George Anson's 1741–45 circumnavigation, 621 of his crew of 960 died.

In 1753 a British naval surgeon, James Lind, published *A Treatise of the Scurvy.* Lind had conducted experiments on a 10-week cruise of the ship *Salisbury.* Twelve sailors with scurvy were given different remedies. The two men who ate a lemon and two oranges a day recovered. Lind thus concluded that scurvy could be prevented with citrus fruits. The Admiralty embraced his theories, and for good reason. Although Anson's campaign in the Pacific had successfully captured Spanish treasure ships, his crew had been hit hard by scurvy. Of the 77 crewmembers on one of his ships, 50 were incapacitated due to scurvy. In order to avoid this sort of catastrophe during the voyage of the *Endeavour,* the Victualling Board of the Admiralty ordered Cook to include in the ship's provisions antiscorbutics, foods that were thought to prevent scurvy. The *Endeavour's* stores included sauerkraut, salted cabbage, malt, orange rob (a sort of orange juice concentrate), and "portable soup." In 1938 chemists studied a slab of 18th-century portable soup and determined that the dehydrated broth was made of meat and bones and that it had not "undergone any marked change in 160 odd years." Although useless as an antiscorbutic, portable soup no doubt nourished Cook's crew and contributed to its remarkably low mortality rate. Until vitamin C could be isolated in tablet form in the 20th century, British ships' stores included plenty of citrus fruits, hence the nickname for an English sailor—"limey."

Cook dictated a particular diet for his men, hoping to avoid the tolls of scurvy and other diseases. Although Cook generally avoided corporal punishment, men who failed to eat their allotment of fresh meat were flogged. As a result of these measures, none of the

Endeavour's crew—or "The People," as Cook called them—perished from disease in the South Pacific.

The *Endeavour*'s first port was Madeira, a Portuguese colony off the east coast of Africa. Water, wine, and fresh food, including a bull for later butchering, were obtained for the journey across the Atlantic Ocean. The ship reached Rio de Janeiro by mid-November, and the expedition aroused the suspicions of the Portuguese governor, Antonio Rolim de Moura. Were these English sailors pirates? Smugglers? Spies? Portugal was desperate to hold on to its colonial territories and, although the *Endeavour* had been welcomed in Madeira, de Moura considered Cook and his crew as representatives of an ambitious rival. The *Endeavour* needed repairs after the long Atlantic passage. Cook was anxious to restock the food supplies before setting out for Tahiti. The sailors were land hungry after two

months at sea. Tense negotiations resulted in provisioning, but the crew remained on board for three weeks in the Brazilian port. Even as the *Endeavour* sailed out of the Rio de Janeiro harbor, the governor ordered shots fired across its bow, a clear sign of de Moura's hostility. It was not an auspicious start for what promised to be a dangerous passage around the tip of South America.

December 11 saw the *Endeavour* sailing along the coast of Tierra del Fuego. Cook had charted a course for the Strait of Le Maire and Cape Horn rather than planning to pass through the Strait of Magellan. As the ship sailed south the climate became frigid. The expedition's first fatalities occurred on December 15 as Joseph Banks led a specimen-collecting party ashore at the Bay of Good Success. Two black men, Richmond and Dorlton, personal servants to Banks, froze to death in an ice storm. Despite this second omen,

In an image drawn by William Hodges, an artist who sailed with Cook, a ship sails along the harsh land of Tierra del Fuego. *(Library of Congress, Prints and Photographs Division [LC-USZ62-77399])*

and despite the increasing cold, the *Endeavour* sailed still farther south. On January 25, 1769, the ship rounded the cape. James Cook first saw the ocean with which his name and destiny would be linked forevermore.

Determined to see what, if anything, lay in the southern latitudes and indulging his independence from Admiralty supervision, Cook piloted the *Endeavour* south as far as the 60th parallel. The sea was rough, the air extremely cold, and the crew became loudly impatient to warm themselves on the balmy sands of South Sea islands. Concluding that the Great Southern Continent was not to be found below South America, Cook set course for Tahiti. By March 1 the *Endeavour* was 560 leagues from the coast of Chile. Cook noted that the sea lacked an obvious current, such that a huge landmass would have caused, and added this evidence to his growing case against the existence of a southern continent.

TAHITI, TAHITIANS, AND THE TRANSIT OF VENUS

On April 13 the *Endeavour* anchored in Matavai Bay, Tahiti. Cook ordered his sailors

By the time of Cook's visit to Tahiti in 1769, its people had become somewhat accustomed to European visitors. This drawing shows Tahitians entertaining Cook. *(National Archives of Canada)*

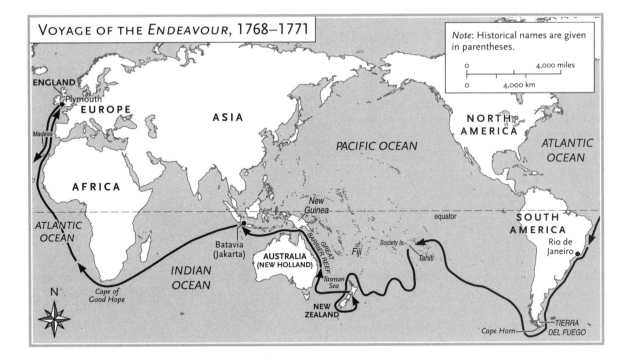

VOYAGE OF THE *ENDEAVOUR*, 1768–1771

Note: Historical names are given in parentheses.

and officers to treat the native people "with every imaginable humanity" as they joyfully disembarked for this fabled tropical paradise. The Tahitians, already accustomed to Europeans by the recent visits of Wallis and Bougainville, were willing to trade and to establish friendly relations with the expedition. Tahitians shared a communal culture that did not recognize private property. Both men and women embraced open sexuality. No obvious king or commander controlled the people. All this puzzled the English. Cook and his crew reported what they disparaged as regular theft of supplies and equipment, including nails from the *Endeavour*'s hull and the astronomical quadrant critical to the measurement of the Transit of Venus, which was later returned. When a party was invited to dinner on shore, Solander's eyeglasses and Banks's snuffbox disappeared. Cook's journal indicates that sexual contacts between his sailors and Tahitian women were frequent, although he disapproved of such relationships. He also later noted that members of his crew contracted venereal diseases, presumably from Tahitian women who in turn had been infected by earlier European visitors. Where Cook was prepared to negotiate with one chief, Tahitian society presented him with many chiefs, or *ari'i*, and every chief was recognized by a complex set of prohibited behaviors, called *tapu*. Cook's detailed descriptions of native cultures encountered during the expeditions were valuable contributions to early anthropology.

Charles Green and Cook observed and measured the Transit of Venus on June 3, 1769, a day so hot—117 degrees Fahrenheit—that touching the instruments was a painful task. The first assignment of the expedition completed, the *Endeavour* sailed from Matavai

Bay on July 13. A Tahitian priest, Tupaia, and a man who was his son or apprentice joined the crew to serve as guides and navigators. Tupaia directed Cook to a group of neighboring islands that Cook christened the Society Islands. Cook carefully charted these islands, as he had Tahiti, before setting out to the west on August 9.

COOK CHARTS NEW ZEALAND

James Cook now opened his second set of orders, kept secret for a year. The *Endeavour* was to search for the southern continent, chart New Zealand, and discover any other unknown lands. Cook, having studied the records of previous voyages of discovery, knew the task was immense and the chance of failure high. Undaunted, he set the course of his ship south yet again.

The *Endeavour* sailed as far south as 40°22', and Cook found no sign of the great continent. Seeking New Zealand, Cook directed the ship west. On October 6, Nicholas Young, the ship's surgeon's boy, earned a gallon of rum for being first to sight land. Two days later the *Endeavour* anchored in a bay Cook named Poverty Bay because no provisions could be gotten there. The native people, probably frightened by the appearance of white people in a great ship, exhibited hostility toward the British. Tupaia was able to serve as an interpreter and diplomat since his language and that of the Maori were strikingly similar. The English regarded the native peoples of New Zealand as less friendly and less civilized than the Tahitians. Their European sensibilities were outraged by the ritual cannibalism that was an important part of Maori warfare and culture.

Its officers giving English names to New Zealand's bays, inlets, and capes, the *Endeav-*

Shown in an 1890s photograph, Tawhiao was a Maori king of New Zealand. *(Library of Congress, Prints and Photographs Division [LC-USZ62-109768])*

our rounded the island and by January 1770 was exploring its western coast. Forays on shore for water, food, and scurvy-preventing grasses convinced Cook and Banks that New Zealand was suitable for settlement by British colonists and was a priceless possession for the Crown. Ship's boats were sent to explore the contours of the bay Cook named Queen Charlotte Sound, after the wife of George III. Cook was surprised to find that the sound led into a passage—the strait now bearing his name—separating New Zealand's two islands; no previous account or map had hinted at this. The *Endeavour* sailed east through the strait and then clockwise around the southern island.

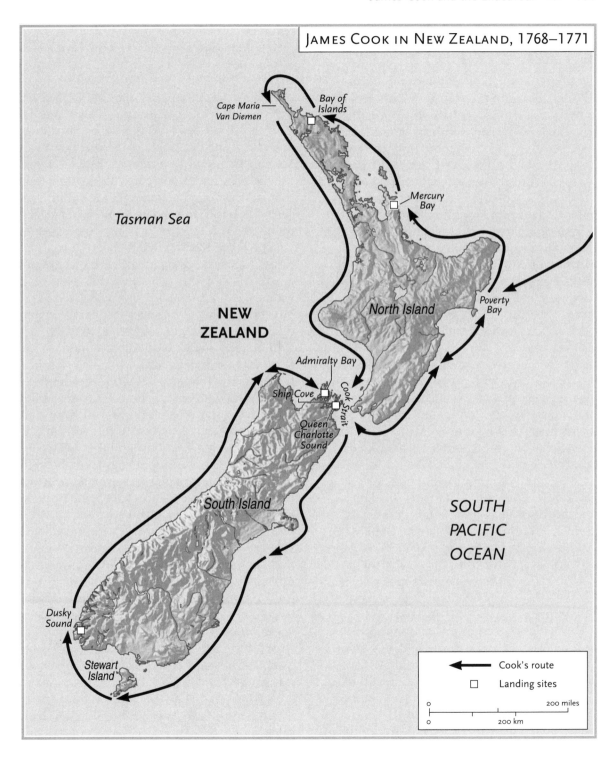

JAMES COOK IN NEW ZEALAND, 1768–1771

Cape Maria
Van Diemen

Bay of
Islands

Mercury
Bay

Tasman Sea

NEW
ZEALAND

North Island

Poverty
Bay

Admiralty Bay

Ship Cove

Cook Strait

Queen
Charlotte
Sound

SOUTH
PACIFIC
OCEAN

South Island

Dusky
Sound

Stewart
Island

Cook's route

Landing sites

0   200 miles

0   200 km

THE *ENDEAVOUR* JOURNEYS HOME

By March, Cook had explored and accurately charted more than 2,400 miles of New Zealand's coast. He had proved that New Zealand was not the fabled southern continent but instead two vast islands, rich in natural resources to be exploited for Great Britain's benefit. The *Endeavour* had addressed and surpassed its orders, and the expedition had only to determine its route back to England. Cook was inclined to further demolish the continental theory by sailing east toward Cape Horn, exploring farther south than he had two years before. But the *Endeavour* was in poor shape, unlikely to weather the rough seas at the bottom of the world. Cook and his officers charted the fastest route home: west to the eastern coast of New Holland, along that coast to its northernmost point, north to the "lands discovered by Quiros" and to Batavia, round the Cape of Good Hope, and then to England.

Though homeward bound, the expedition continued to be one of exploration. The *Endeavour* anchored April 29 at a bay near present-day Sydney. Banks found so many unique and fascinating plant species that he dubbed it Botany Bay. This bay was to become the legendary main port of immigration to the British colony, New Holland. Cook sailed north, charting 2,000 miles of New Holland's eastern coast. Heading for New Guinea, on June 10, 1770, the *Endeavour* made an accidental, and nearly fatal, landing on the Great Barrier Reef.

Already in compromised condition, with rotting timbers and a fragile hull, the *Endeavour* stuck fast and seemed certain to be torn apart by the coral daggers of the reef. Ballast, anchors, and cannons were thrown overboard in a desperate effort to lighten the ship so it could float free. Below deck, the sea poured in.

Sailors pumped frantically, but the water was faster than they were. Cook remained calm, directing his crew masterfully, and hoping that the *Endeavour* would be lifted from the reef. His private thoughts were dark, however, and he wrote in his journal, "This was an alarming and I may say terrible circumstance and threatened immediate destruction to us as soon as the ship was afloat." After 23 hours on the reef, the *Endeavour* did indeed float free, but damage was severe. A sailor suggested that the largest hole in the ship's hull be mended by fothering, a tricky maneuver in which a sail stuffed with sheep dung and tarred ropes was dragged under the ship until it was sucked into the hole and formed a watertight plug. The attempt was successful, but the *Endeavour* was severely crippled and made for land, any land, immediately.

The crew made all possible repairs to the ship, leaving a coral stake piercing the hull rather than attempting to patch another hole. The *Endeavour* was barely seaworthy when it sailed from the northeast coast of New Holland on August 6. Once again the perils of the Great Barrier Reef lay between the *Endeavour* and home. Cook cautiously guided the ship through the reef and then charted a northeast course, testing the notion that New Holland and New Guinea were joined. Desperate to find a strait whose existence he only guessed at, and whose existence would greatly shorten the journey to Batavia, Cook guided the *Endeavour* slightly south of the Strait of Torres. On October 10 the *Endeavour* limped into Batavia's harbor, its sails so ragged, Cook wrote, "they will hardly stand the least puff of wind." When the rest of the ship was examined, carpenters discovered that in some places the planking on the hull had worn to one-eighth of an inch thickness and that most of the critical timbers were thoroughly worm-ridden.

Cook's regime of fresh food, sanitation, and hygiene had prevented sickness to a remarkable extent during the long voyage. Only four or five crewmembers had been touched by scurvy, and none had died of disease. This luck was not to last. Batavia was known to be unhealthy, surrounded by swamps and peopled by itinerant sailors and traders whose commerce was not only spice but also germs. Within weeks of landing in Batavia, seven crewmembers were dead, including ship's surgeon, William Monkhouse, and both Tahitians. Forty men were seriously ill from malaria and dysentery. All were weak with tropical fevers. Cook feared more deaths and determined to leave as soon as the *Endeavour* could be prepared. Between Batavia and the Cape of Good Hope, 22 more men perished.

On July 10 the *Endeavour* came within sight of Land's End. Three days later Cook reported to the Admiralty in London. His achievements in discovery remain unsurpassed. The expedition charted more than 5,000 coastal miles. Cook established the position and features of remote lands with more precision and detail than was to be found on

Cook brought many cultural artifacts from his journeys in the Pacific Ocean to England when he returned. These carvings, photographed in the 1890s, are by the Maori of New Zealand and include small and large figures of gods, as well as canoe paddles. *(Library of Congress, Prints and Photographs Division [LC-D4271-735])*

many contemporary maps of Europe. Thousands of important biological specimens were made available to scientists. Ethnographic descriptions and drawings of the peoples of the South Pacific, New Zealand, and New Holland partly countered European fantasies about savages and cannibals. Paintings and drawings of the new lands and their inhabitants gave life to the written accounts. Great Britain now had fair claim to greater territory in the Pacific than any other European power. And, at least to Cook and his supporters, the Great Southern Continent was proven at last to be myth.

James Cook added a postscript to his journal of the *Endeavour*'s three-year voyage, seeking to impress upon his Royal Navy superiors the unbounded opportunities for further exploration in the South Pacific. "Now I am upon the subject of discoveries I hope it will not be taken a Miss if I give it as my opinion that the most feasible Method of making fu[r]ther discoveries in the South Sea," Cook wrote, "is to enter it by the way of New Zeland." He continued, describing an expedition of such thoroughness that "thus the discoveries in the South Sea would be compleat."

9

COOK'S PACIFIC

The men of the *Endeavour* were hailed as heroes in Great Britain. Cook received a promotion. On August 14, 1771, he was presented to King George III as Commander James Cook. Joseph Banks exhibited his collections of plants, animal specimens, and artifacts such as tapa cloths, carvings, and weapons. The Admiralty, perhaps doubting the literary talents of a former able-bodied seaman, arranged for Cook's journals to be edited by popular writer John Hawkesworth. Cook was displeased with the artistic flourishes Hawkesworth added, but the three volumes—complete with maps, engravings, and the record of Samuel Wallis's expedition—sold out immediately, and a second edition was hurried into print. Newspapers had been full of colorful stories of Wallis's days in Tahiti, including the invention of a romance between a Tahitian princess and the captain. Cook's discoveries were similarly sensationalized. To the British public the South Pacific truly was an earthly paradise. Surely the Great Southern Continent, the land of Solomon's riches, would be located within its reaches.

In France, Louis-Antoine de Bougainville's voyage and the published accounts of the South Seas elicited a similar response. Expeditions were immediately organized to reinforce France's claims to the lands Bougainville had visited. As Bougainville sailed back to France from the Pacific, Jean-François-Marie du Surville was calling at ports of trade in India and China with his ship *St. Jean Baptiste*. News of the Wallis, Philip Carteret, and Bougainville expeditions were carried from ship to ship, from Batavia to Cochin, on the Indian coast. Surville sailed south to investigate the rumors he had heard about the great southern land sought by the expeditions. Surville sailed through the Solomons but got lost in the Coral Sea. The *St. Jean Baptiste*, quite by accident, found its way to New Zealand by the middle of December 1769. The *Endeavour* and the *St. Jean Baptiste* probably came within a few miles of each other.

In 1771, Marc-Joseph Marion, sieur du Fresne, was sent to find Terra Australis Incognita. Bougainville himself paid for the expedition because one part of its mission was to return Ahu-Toru to his home in Tahiti. Ahu-Toru died of smallpox before Marion's ships, the *Mascarin* and the *Castries*, could reach Tahiti. With his passenger gone, Marion decided to sail south in search of the southern continent. Marion, like Surville, more or less wandered to New Zealand. In June 1772, as his men watched in horror, Marion was killed in a battle with Maori warriors.

Sailing from Mauritius in January 1772, Frenchman Yves-Joseph Kerguélen-Trémarec drove 2,000 miles to the south looking for the southern continent. When he found land at 50° south latitude, Kerguélen felt certain it was part of this continent and named it New France. Frigid cold and rough seas prevented thorough exploration, and the *Fortune* and the *Gros Ventre*, Kerguélen's ships, returned to Mauritius. When Kerguélen went back to New France the next year, he investigated far enough to realize he had found a large, isolated island. He changed its name to Desolation Land.

Spain, concerned that French and British activities in the Pacific would restrict its trade in the Philippines, sent its ships into the Pacific. In 1770, Felipé González landed at Easter Island and claimed it for Spain. He renamed it San Carlos to honor his king, (Charles) III. The Spanish viceroy of Peru, Manuel de Amat y Jumient, declared that Spain still owned all the territories in the Pacific under the terms of Vasco Nuñez de Balboa's 1513 claim. In 1772, Amat sent Domingo Boenechea to Tahiti to determine whether the British had settled colonists there. Boenechea's ship, the *Aquila*, anchored in Matavai Bay for a month. Finding no evidence of a permanent British presence, Boenechea claimed Tahiti for Spain.

GREAT BRITAIN SENDS A SECOND EXPEDITION IN SEARCH OF THE SOUTHERN CONTINENT

Great Britain had good intelligence about the French and Spanish forays into the Pacific and determined to send its ships once more in search of Terra Australis Incognita. Alexander Dalrymple, who himself hoped to command such an expedition, wrote to the Royal Society urging further exploration. He offered his argument that Quirós had reached the southern continent as proof that explorers since simply had failed to search in the right place. Cook doubted that Quirós had ever found Terra Australis Incognita, but he agreed that, since no known ships had sailed in the far South Pacific, there was a slight chance the southern continent would be found there. He accepted an assignment from the Admiralty to search for the continent to, as he later wrote, "put an end to all diversity of opinion about a matter so curious and important."

Cook, mindful of the *Endeavour*'s struggle on the Great Barrier Reef, asked the Admiralty to supply him with smaller, more maneuverable ships. He asked for colliers once again, large enough to carry sufficient provisions but small enough that their crews could haul them onshore for repairs. Cook would be the captain of the flagship *Resolution*. Tobias Furneaux, who had served with Wallis on the *Dolphin*, had the helm of the *Adventure*. Joseph Banks planned a grand floating scientific experiment, hiring 16 naturalists and artists and suggesting alterations to the ships to accommodate his staff. Cook refused to make changes that he thought would destabilize the *Resolution*, and Banks withdrew from the enterprise entirely.

Scientific exploration remained a critical part of Cook's plans, and Johann Reinhold Forster became the expedition's naturalist. Forster, in *Observations Made during a Voyage around the World*, wrote, "My object was nature in its greatest extent, the Earth, the Sea, the Air, the Organic and Animated Creation, and more particularly that class of Beings to

This cartoon satirizes Joseph Banks's fame after the *Endeavour* expedition. The cartoon shows his metamorphosis from a caterpillar into a butterfly. *(Library of Congress, Prints and Photographs Division [LC-USZC4-8780])*

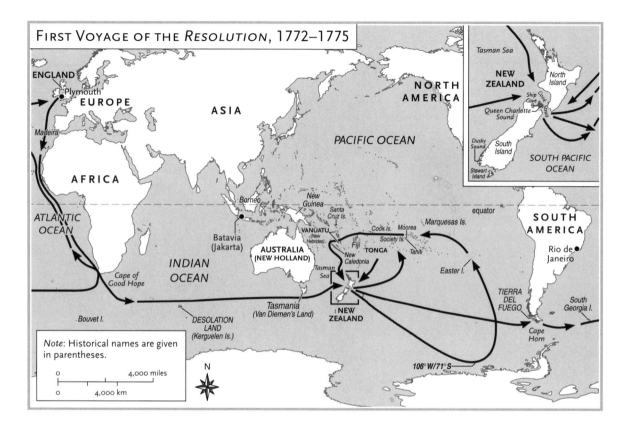

FIRST VOYAGE OF THE *RESOLUTION*, 1772–1775

which we ourselves belong." Artist William Hodges would accompany Forster and record many of his discoveries. William Bayly, accompanied by fellow astronomer William Wales, brought a "portable observatory" on board. The Admiralty expected them to observe, measure, and record eclipses and all other astronomical events. The Board of Longitude, a Parliamentary commission, had recently awarded £10,000 to John Harrison for his invention of an accurate ship's chronometer. Cook's ships were the first to carry these instruments, which enabled precise calculation of longitude. Cook was instructed by the Astronomer Royal Nevil Maskelyne, "you are particularly to exert your Best Endeavour to settle the Longitude of the Cape of good Hope with the utmost accuracy."

Cook's plan was to enter the Pacific by way of the Cape of Good Hope. His ships would then sail south of the cape to 54° south latitude in hopes of finding Cape Circumcision, first reported by Frenchman Jean-Baptiste-Charles Bouvet de Lozier in 1739. Bouvet thought this land, which now bears his name, might be the northern tip of the southland. If Cook determined that it was an island, he would proceed as far south as his ships and men would bear and then sail east. In effect, Cook would circumnavigate the Earth's most southern latitudes.

The *Resolution* and the *Adventure* left Plymouth on July 13, 1772, and anchored at Cape Town in late October to take on provisions. Sailing south a month later, the ships never saw Cape Circumcision as they ventured into the freezing southern latitudes. Ice covered the riggings, and snow drifted on the decks. The crew was issued heavy woolen clothing called dreadnoughts. By the middle of December, Cook's men were keeping watch for icebergs night and day. Floating islands of ice 50

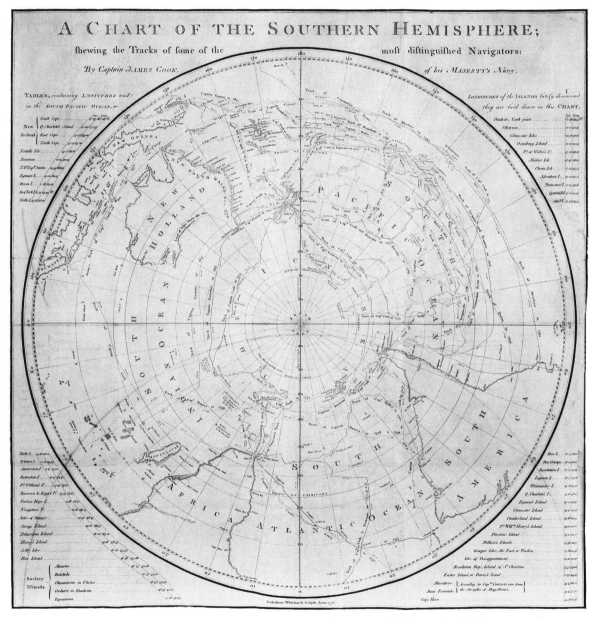

Captain James Cook drew this map of the Southern Hemisphere, on which he included the routes of many famous explorers. *(Library of Congress, Prints and Photographs Division [LC-USZ62-77400])*

feet high and two miles long threatened to crush the ships. Cook wrote in his log that the ice "conveyed to the mind a coldness, much greater than it was." Smaller pieces of floating ice were hauled onboard and melted to supply fresh water. On January 17, 1773, shortly before midnight, the *Resolution* and the *Adventure* became the first ships to enter the Antarctic Circle.

Just south of the Circle, at 67° south latitude, the ice became so treacherous that Cook turned his ships north and proceeded east just above the Antarctic Circle. Sailing with 20 hours of sunlight each day, Cook pushed his ships east. On February 17 the men witnessed the Aurora Australis, the southern lights. Cook recorded, "Last night lights were seen in the Heavens . . . I do not remember of any Voyagers making mention of them being seen in the Southern [hemisphere] before." Shortly after this, the *Adventure* disappeared in a fog. Cook and Furneaux had made arrangements to meet at Queen Charlotte Sound in New Zealand if the ships became separated. Unconcerned, Cook continued to sail in the high latitudes until March.

As the antarctic winter began, the *Resolution* sailed north toward New Zealand. Cook anchored in Dusky Bay and permitted his men almost two months of recuperation at the sound. William Bayly set up his observatory. Johann Forster spent the months collecting plant specimens, including the spruce fir that the sailors used to brew scurvy-fighting tea and beer. Forster also discovered 38 new species of birds, which William Hodges sketched and painted.

When the *Resolution* entered Queen Charlotte Sound on May 18, 1773, the *Adventure* was waiting. Furneaux reported that his ship had explored the coast of Van Diemen's land while the *Resolution* sailed in the high latitudes. Cook had planned to winter at

Queen Charlotte Sound, but his stay at Dusky Sound had made him restless to put to sea once more. His plan was to sail for 3,000 miles east at the highest latitude that his men and ships could withstand. If they did not come upon Terra Australis Incognita, the ships would turn north for Tahiti, winter there, and try the high latitudes the following summer. Cook left Queen Charlotte Sound in early June.

COOK RETURNS TO TAHITI

As the expedition sailed east into rough winter seas, a sailor on the *Adventure* died of scurvy. Twenty more were very ill. Cook was enraged; he had ordered the scurvy-fighting diet that had kept the men of the *Endeavour* healthy be followed on both ships. Few men on Cook's ships enjoyed the menu. One, Alexander Home, included his complaints in his journal, "for God's sake that he [Cook] be obleged to Eat such Damned Stuff." To Cook, the appearance of scurvy on Furneaux's ship indicated poor leadership and discipline. The condition of the *Adventure*'s men and colder weather than he anticipated led Cook to change course and head to Tahiti. The ships anchored at Matavai Bay on August 25.

The British were warmly greeted as old friends, but Cook was troubled by the changes he saw on the island. Tahiti was not the same untouched paradise he had visited four years before. European tools and household items were widely used. Fair-haired children with Caucasian features ran laughing along the beach. His Tahitian friends told Cook that guns had been given to them by the Spanish and were used in feuds with neighboring islands. A Spanish deserter was rumored to be living somewhere in Tahiti's interior. Most distressing, Cook found the island's population noticeably smaller. Sexually transmitted diseases and influenza had killed many Tahitians in a short time.

The *Resolution* and the *Adventure* sailed from Matavai Bay on September 17, 1773. Cook wanted to make sure they could reach the high southern latitudes during the warm season. Tobias Furneaux invited a man from Huahine, in the Society Islands, Omai, to join the crew of the *Adventure* as a guide. As the ships sailed toward New Zealand, Omai pointed out islands—Tonga and what are now called the Cook group—that Cook had never before seen. On October 21 the *Adventure* disappeared again. When Furneaux's ship failed to rendezvous at Ship Cove as arranged, Cook waited two weeks for his other ship. Then, worried about being too late in the season to sail safely in the high latitudes, Cook left a message for Furneaux in a bottle buried and marked with a stake. In late November the *Resolution* sailed once more to the south.

The *Adventure* put into Ship Cove only a few days after Cook left. Furneaux had followed what he thought to be the *Resolution*'s course south. In December the *Adventure* arrived in Queen Charlotte Sound and engaged in a battle with the local Maoris. Eight of the *Adventure*'s men were killed and

This illustration depicts Captain Cook escaping in a rowboat from native inhabitants during a voyage in the Pacific Ocean. The native people's reception of Captain Cook and his crew varied from island to island, depending partly on those people's past experiences with European visitors. *(Library of Congress, Prints and Photographs Division [LC-USZ62-102093])*

This 1922 photograph shows Tahitians gathered around a sailboat. Captain James Cook first visited the island in 1769. *(Library of Congress, Prints and Photographs Division [LC-USZ62-111979])*

their corpses cannibalized. The traumatized men of the *Adventure* decided to return to England as quickly as possible. Furneaux sailed his ship around Cape Horn, then crossed the Atlantic to the Cape of Good Hope. After refitting the *Adventure* at Table Bay, Furneaux journeyed north and arrived in England in July 1774. The *Adventure* had become the first ship to circumnavigate the globe west to east.

The *Resolution* sailed to latitude 67° south in December. Again ice coated its rigging, and snow covered its decks. The sails froze, and Cook's men had difficulty adjusting them. Cook devised a strategy to explore as much ocean as possible while getting occasional relief from the cold. The *Resolution* zigzagged, going southeast until the cold was unbearable and then sailing northeast to latitude 48° south to thaw his crew and ship. In this manner Cook reached longitude 106° west, latitude 71° south in the last days of 1773. The *Resolution* was only a few miles from the coast of Antarctica. Cold and ice prevented Cook from actually seeing the continent, but he had decided by this time that the fabled Terra Australis Incognita was a barren continent of ice and rock at the bottom of the world.

Since the *Resolution* was just below South America, Cook could easily have sailed to Cape Horn and then home to England. Instead, he determined to see more of the Pacific. He wrote in his journal, "I was of the opinion that my remaining in this sea some time longer would be productive of some improvements to navigation and geography as well as other sciences."

Cook set out for Easter Island, arriving there on March 11, 1774. He unfavorably compared the sparse landscape of the island to the lushness of Tahiti, but found the people to be physically very similar to the Tahitians and Maoris. The massive stone heads he saw amazed Cook. Forster speculated they had been carved by an ancient, more sophisticated culture. William Hodges painted the statues, providing Europeans with their first images of the mysterious stones. From Easter Island the *Resolution* set course for Tahiti. Cook hoped he would find the *Adventure* there.

On April 6, the ship approached the Marquesas, the first European ships to visit since Álvaro de Mendaña in 1595. Cook charted the Marquesas and explored their shores. Once again he remarked on the physical resemblance the islanders bore to the Tahitians and noted that patterns on Marquesan cloth and in Marquesan tattoos were almost identical to ones he had seen on Tahiti.

When the *Resolution* arrived in Matavai Bay on April 22, the Tahitians were preparing for war with neighboring Moorea. Fascinated by Tahitian war canoes, Cook recorded fleets of as many as 150 boats. He measured canoes as big as 90 feet long. After six weeks, and no sign of the *Adventure*, Cook set his next destination: the islands where Quirós had established his short-lived colony in 1606. Espíritu Santo was 3,000 miles away. Cook planned to chart the islands and return to New Zealand to prepare the *Resolution* for its voyage home.

In July, Cook charted Quirós's islands in detail. He gave them an English name, the New Hebrides; they are now called Vanuatu. While the *Resolution* was in Vanuatu some of its men fired their guns at islanders they perceived as menacing. Cook captured the dilemma that many Europeans and islanders had faced over the previous two centuries: "It is impossible for them to know our design. We enter these parts and attempt to land in a peaceable manner. If this succeeds, all is well. If not, we land nonetheless and maintain our footing by the superiority of our firearms. In what other light can they first look upon us but as invaders of their country?"

In late October 1774 the *Resolution* sailed to New Zealand's Ship Cove. On his way south Cook found and charted the large island of New Caledonia as well as numerous smaller islands. Having explored 60,000 miles of the Pacific, Cook prepared for the voyage home. Its crew overhauled the *Resolution* and gathered fuel, wood, and water to sustain them until they reached Cape Horn. Some Maori traders told Cook of a great battle in which white men had been killed the year before. Cook then learned at least something of the fate of the *Adventure*.

The *Resolution* left Ship Cove on November 11 and sailed east to Cape Horn, where the men celebrated Christmas. Cook could not resist the possibility of one more discovery. As the *Resolution* sailed toward the Cape of Good Hope, he turned it south into the high latitudes one more time. He found icy South Georgia Island and claimed it for Great Britain. On July 30, 1775, after three years at sea, the *Resolution* anchored at Spithead, England. Cook wrote in his journal, "I have now done with the Southern Pacific Continent, and flatter myself that no one will think I have left it unexplored."

COOK'S THIRD VOYAGE

More celebrated than before, James Cook was promoted to Post-Captain upon his return. Captain Cook was made a Fellow of the Royal Society and presented a paper entitled "The Method Taken for Preserving the Health of the Crew of His Majesty's Ship the *Resolution* during her Late Voyage around the World." The Society awarded him its most prestigious honor, the William Copley Medal, for his work in preventing scurvy on his ships. The Royal Society and the Admiralty had a new project

for Cook but, as on his first voyage, his orders were to be kept secret. The British very much wanted to resolve the other great geographical puzzle of the age. Cook was to go to North America and search for a passage through the continent that would link the Pacific and the

In this illustration by John Webber, inhabitants of Ha'apai, one of the Tonga Islands, prepare a reception for Captain Cook. *(Library of Congress, Prints and Photographs Division [LC-USZ62-102238])*

Atlantic. Great Britain's investments in China and interests in the Pacific fur industry would become even more valuable if its ships could quickly cross North America. With Britain's American colonies in rebellion, the motive for increased revenues was strong.

Cook sailed from Plymouth in the refitted *Resolution* on July 12, 1776. A companion ship, the *Discovery*, would join Cook's flagship in Cape Town. Artist John Webber accompanied the expedition, as did botanist David Nelson, who was to collect plant specimens

While Cook was visiting Tahiti during his third voyage, he found out that the islanders were fighting with the inhabitants of nearby Moorea. In this engraving by John Webber, the Tahitians sacrifice humans and pigs to appease Oro, the god of war. *(Library of Congress, Prints and Photographs Division [LC-USZ62-102230])*

for the Royal Botanic Gardens at Kew, just outside London. Astronomer William Bayly was appointed by the Board of Longitude to set out with Cook once again. The master of the *Resolution* was William Bligh; he would become better known as the captain of HMS *Bounty.* Also on the *Resolution* was Omai, who had sailed to England on Cook's second voyage. One public justification for the expedition was to bring Omai back to Huahine in Tahiti after his two years as an English celebrity.

The *Discovery,* captained by Charles Clerke, met the *Resolution* at Cape Town as scheduled. On December 1, the two ships sailed south. Cook wanted to see Kerguélen's Desolation Land. He had been given a chart to the region by a Frenchman the year before in Cape Town and wanted to check its accuracy. Cook's ships spent Christmas Day at Kerguélen's island and found a bottle containing a parchment that recorded visits by French ships in 1772 and 1773.

Sailing north, Cook made his only landing at Van Diemen's Land and on February 11, 1777, arrived at what he called "our old station," Queen Charlotte Sound. Cook followed what had become a routine. His ships were repaired, and provisions were gathered. After two weeks the *Resolution* and the *Discovery* sailed north from New Zealand. On this voyage Cook allowed more time to explore the islands around Tahiti. For five months, the *Resolution* and the *Discovery* meandered through Tonga, which Cook called the Friendly Islands.

Arriving at Tahiti on August 11, the ships moored at Vaitepina Bay. Cook learned that missionaries from Peru had visited during his absence and saw remnants of their mission and a large cross they had erected. Tahiti was at war with Moorea, and Cook and his men were invited to witness a human sacrifice to Oro, the god of war. Cook wrote this was, "a good opportunity to see something of this extraordinary and Barbarous custom."

Cook saw Tahiti for the last time on September 29, 1777, as his ships sailed for the

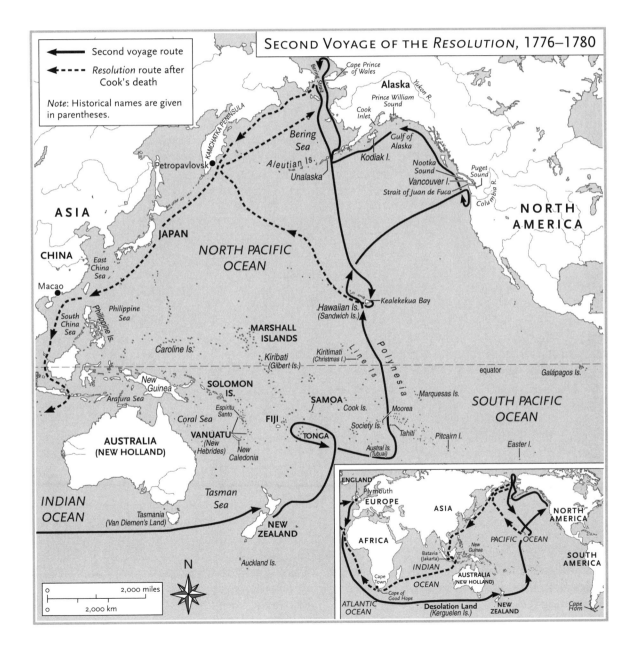

SECOND VOYAGE OF THE *RESOLUTION*, 1776–1780

→ Second voyage route

◄---- *Resolution* route after Cook's death

Note: Historical names are given in parentheses.

Society Islands. The expedition spent the next eight weeks charting Huahine, where Omai was reunited with his family and community, Moorea, and Ra'iatea. By early December, Cook was ready to set course for the coast of North America.

FARTHER THAN ANY MAN

The Admiralty had ordered Cook to explore the coast of New Albion, the part of northern California Francis Drake had visited during the reign of Elizabeth I. To reach New Caledonia from Tahiti, the *Resolution* and the *Discovery* had to traverse thousands of miles of uncharted ocean. The ships first found an anchorage on December 24 at a small island

they named Christmas. A week was spent replenishing provisions and celebrating the holidays. Leaving Christmas Island on January 2, 1778, the ships sailed about two weeks, and the lookout saw a group of islands on the horizon on January 18.

The island's inhabitants saw sails approaching and paddled out in canoes to greet the ships. The *Resolution* and the *Discovery* were the first European ships to enter Hawaii's waters. Cook named the previously unknown islands the Sandwich Islands, in honor of his patron, John Montagu, earl of Sandwich. The ships anchored off the island of Kauai and spent two weeks with the Hawaiians, who provided the ships with welcome food and water. Cook was able to communicate with the peo-

Originally published in a late 18th-century book about James Cook's voyages, this engraving by John Webber, who accompanied Cook on his third voyage, depicts Chukchi people on the Bering Sea and their dwellings. *(Library of Congress, Prints and Photographs Division [LC-USZ62-102229])*

The Northwest Passage ∼

Ever since the third century B.C., when Greek explorer Pythias claimed to have journeyed to an island in the far north, Europeans had clung to the idea that a northern water passage to the East existed almost as tenaciously as they believed in the existence of a Great Southern Continent. The discovery of such a passage was important because it would presumably be a safer route to the riches of the East. Trading ships would avoid Spanish and Portuguese warships, and it was hoped that a northern passage would be free from the storms that made sailing around the Capes of Good Hope and Horn so treacherous.

Early explorers looked in vain for a northeast passage over the European continent. John Cabot, an Italian sailor commanded by England's king Henry VII, predicted during his 1497 explorations of the North Atlantic that a Northwest Passage would be found in North America. Frenchman Jacques Cartier concluded in 1534 that such a route did not go *through* North America. Englishman Martin Frobisher's study of the northern American coast in 1576–78 convinced many, including Francis Drake, that the Northwest Passage would be found above the continent. A Greek pilot sailing for Spain and taking a Spanish name, Juan de Fuca, claimed he had actually found the passage in 1592, but it was only the strait now named for him.

Russians carried on much of the early exploration of the North Pacific as they sought a western approach to the passage. Vitus Bering, a Dane in the service of Czar Peter I the Great, discovered the strait that bears his name while searching for the Northwest Passage in 1724. British explorers continued the search as late as 1792, when George Vancouver hoped to include it on his masterful charts of the west coast of North America. The fledgling United States inherited Britain's great desire to link North American colonies to the Orient by finding the Northwest Passage. In 1804, President Thomas Jefferson sent Meriwether Lewis and William Clark on an expedition up the Missouri River in search of the passage.

By the 19th century large clipper ships could sail with relative ease around Cape Horn into the Pacific, and the search for the Northwest Passage became of less commercial interest than scientific. Several expeditions set out to discover the passage. Some ended in disaster. John Franklin led 129 men to an icebound death during an 1845 British expedition. Efforts to rescue that expedition, however, led to good evidence that the passage actually existed in a 900-mile route, 500 miles north of the Arctic Circle. Norwegian Roald Amundsen became the first explorer to successfully travel the passage, from 1903–06.

ple on Kauai, as their language was very similar to that of the Tahitians.

On February 3 the *Resolution* and the *Discovery* left Hawaii and sailed for New Albion.

They reached the North American coast at present-day Oregon the first week of March. The ships sailed north from a headland Cook named Cape Foul Weather, charting each geographic feature as they followed the Pacific Northwest coast of America. On March 29 the expedition entered Nootka Sound on the western side of Vancouver Island. A Spanish explorer, Juan Peréz, had been sent from Mexico four years earlier to investigate fur-trading

Mark Twain on the Death of Captain Cook ⌒

Mark Twain (the pen name of Samuel Langhorne Clemens, 1835–1910) was sent to the Sandwich Islands by the San Francisco *Union* as a traveling correspondent in 1866. Steamship service between San Francisco and Honolulu had just begun, and Americans were deeply invested in the sugar trade with the Hawaiian Islands. Visiting Maui, Oahu, and Hawaii, and studying all sorts of sources of life in Hawaii—from Hawaiian-language phrasebooks and newspapers to court records and government reports—Twain sent 25 articles back to California. Many of his observations were included in lectures Twain gave all over America and incorporated into his 1872 books, *Roughing It*.

Curiosity about the islands was high among Twain's readership and rosy visions about this tropical paradise were popular in an age of American expansion. Twain intended to set the record straight, especially about the great hero James Cook, whose death had been mythologized into a romantic tragedy. Visiting Kealakekua Bay, Twain was brought to the site of Cook's martyrdom. He

wrote, "Plain unvarnished truth takes the romance out of Captain Cook's assassination, and renders it a deliberate verdict of justifiable homicide. Wherever he went among the islands he was cordially received and welcomed by the inhabitants and his ships lavishly supplied with all manner of food. He returned these kindnesses with insult and ill-treatment."

Mark Twain wrote 25 articles about life in Hawaii as a correspondent for the San Francisco *Union*. *(Library of Congress, Prints and Photographs Division [LC-USZ62-112065])* possibilities in the northern Pacific. The people of Nootka Sound were not uncomfortable with the British sailors, and friendly trade was conducted during the month Cook spent in Nootka Sound refitting his ships. John Webber made many fine drawings of the sound and its inhabitants.

In late April the *Resolution* and the *Discovery* left Nootka Sound and sailed north along the coast of Alaska to Prince William Sound, which was investigated and found not to be the Northwest Passage. Cook's men saw whales, walruses, and seals. As they visited Inuit villages, the sailors would exchange knives and mirrors for furs. At the end of May the ships sailed east of Kodiak Island into a promising inlet. For two weeks the expedition sailed through its waters, charting as they went. It, too, proved not to be the passage. Still, Cook gave his name to the inlet.

From Cook Inlet the ships sailed east along the Aleutian island chain, stopping at Unalaska in the Fox group. On August 19, 1778, Cook reached the westernmost point of North America, which he named Cape Prince of Wales. The next day he landed on the Asian continent on the shores of Siberia. The *Resolution* and the *Discovery* passed through the Bering Strait and into the Bering Sea. Cook had sailed as far as 70°44' north latitude when a wall of ice appeared before the ships. The ships turned around, crossed the Bering Sea, and passed through the strait. Looking for fuel and water, Cook searched the Asian shore but found none. The ships returned to Alaska and anchored at Unalaska on October 3. Russian fur traders had worked in the Aleutians since Vitus Bering claimed them for Russia in the 1730s. The official who controlled the region's fur trade, Gerassim Ismailov, and Cook shared their hand-drawn charts of the region.

Cook had thought to spend the winter in Asia at a sheltered point on the Kamchatka Peninsula, from which he would either begin his voyage home by sailing the Asian coast or return to the Bering Sea in search of the Northwest Passage. His men pressed him to return to Hawaii for the winter months, and Cook agreed. In late November the island of Kauai came into view. The ships sailed around the seven islands of Hawaii and in mid-January 1779 entered Kealakekua Bay on the island of Hawaii. Hundreds of canoes with thousands of people welcomed the ships. Two chiefs, Palea and Kanina, and a priest, Koa, came aboard the *Resolution*. Cook went ashore with them and was given a ritual reception in which the island's chief, Kalani'op-u'a, presented him with a cloak of feathers. The expedition had arrived during the Makahiki, a festival honoring the god Lono. Although legend has it that the Hawaiians thought Cook was the reincarnation of Lono, recent historical and anthropological evidence suggest that the arrival of the ships was seen as an auspicious sign and that Cook was celebrated according to island custom.

After the initial festivities Cook's men settled in for the winter. William Bayly set up his observatory, the sailors traded with the Hawaiians, and Cook sent the ships' boats to explore and chart the waters around Hawaii. Within days, tensions began to arise. The presence of the British had disrupted life on Hawaii, and the demands by the British for provisions had strained its economy. Chiefs who visited the British camp began to ask when they were planning to sail away. Cook, not wishing to offend the Hawaiians, made plans to leave. On February 4 the *Resolution* and the *Discovery* sailed from Kealakekua Bay toward Maui. They encountered very strong winds that cracked the foremast of the *Resolution* and forced the ships back into Kealakekua Bay a week later. When Cook went ashore he realized that the Hawaiians did not come to the beach to meet him. A landing party walked inland and still did not see anyone. When Cook's men reached a village, they were told that Kalani'opu'a had gone to another island and had declared the bay *tabu*.

On February 13, Kalani'opu'a returned and came to the British camp. First Lieutenant James Burney of the *Discovery* wrote later, "He was very inquisitive, as were several of the Owhyhe chiefs, to know the reason of our return, and appeared much dissatisfied by it." That night a small boat belonging to the *Discovery* was stolen. On the morning of February 14 stone-throwing islanders attacked a watering party. Cook joined an armed party lead by William Bligh and went ashore to take Kalani'opu'a hostage until the boat was returned. As Cook and his men led the chief to the landing boat, a Hawaiian runner spread the word that the British had killed Kalani'opu'a. An angry crowd rushed to the beach. Cook ordered his men into the boat and before he could do so himself, he was clubbed and stabbed to death.

Stunned by Cook's death, Charles Clerke took charge of the expedition. He had the men make quick repairs to the *Resolution*'s mast. He sent Lieutenant James King, who had best maintained relations with the Hawaiians, to go ashore and retrieve Cook's remains. Most

important, Clerke restrained his men from seeking revenge. On February 22 the *Resolution* and the *Discovery* sailed from Kealakekua Bay.

Clerke directed the ships west and north, to Petropavlovsk in the Kamchatka Peninsula. In April, Clerke gave Cook's journals and charts to a Russian official there, who promised that they would be sent to England. The Admiralty received the papers in December, and Cook's death was widely mourned in Great Britain. Clerke, suffering from tuberculosis, was determined to carry out Cook's mission. On June 13 the *Resolution* and the *Discovery*, which was now captained by John Gore, sailed for the Bering Sea. The expedition was unable to sail any farther north than it had the previous year, and they returned to Petropavlovsk. Clerke died there on August 22, 1779.

John Gore assumed command of the expedition. The *Resolution* and the *Discovery* sailed down the Asian coast to the trading center at Macao, where the sailors sold the furs they had acquired in Alaska at a healthy profit. From China the *Resolution* and the *Discovery* sailed through the islands of Java and Sumatra. By early May they had rounded the Cape of Good Hope. Not until October 1780 did the men who sailed with Cook on his longest voyage see England.

10

SCIENCE AND EMPIRE

James Cook and his men spent four years at sea largely unaware of the great changes taking place on land. Great Britain was at war with its American colonies between 1775 and 1782. When Britain and the United States negotiated a final peace treaty in 1783, a new nation with an old maritime history was poised to become a global power. Britain turned its colonial ambitions to the land France, the Netherlands, Portugal, and Spain had all declined to claim: New Holland. In 1788, Great Britain began to send shiploads of convicts and other undesirables to its colony of New South Wales. With Britain's defeat in the American War of Independence, France regained some of the colonial possessions it had lost during the Seven Years' War. France's navy was well trained, well equipped, and well led. Louis XVI was anxious to return his country to economic stability and world leadership. Although Spain's presence in the Pacific had been declining for two centuries, its colonial officials continued to control the Pacific coast of America. Russia dominated the northern Pacific, establishing colonies in the Aleutian Islands and mainland Alaska.

Exploration of the Pacific over the four previous centuries had produced thousands of maps and charts. At the dawn of the 19th century European and American maps showed most of the ocean's islands and coasts. Cook had proved that the Great Southern Continent was a myth, although one that had inspired much discovery. Trade remained a powerful incentive for expeditions to the Pacific. The center for trade moved north from the East Indies to China and Thailand. Cargoes of tea, silk, furs, porcelains, and opium were loaded onto ships to the ports of Siam and Canton, bound for London and New England.

Whale oil and sealskins replaced cloves and nutmeg as the most desired products of the Pacific. Ships searching for furs and oil also found islands, more than 50 of them during the 19th century. Whaling and trading vessels required accurate charts, and the need to refine the maps made by earlier expeditions drove much of 19th-century exploration efforts in the Pacific. As whales were killed in greater numbers, whaling voyages would venture farther and farther into the ocean to seek remaining schools. Trips could extend from three to five years. These ships also needed ports in which they could warehouse cargo during their long voyages, broker their cargoes, and refuel. Papeete in Tahiti and Lahaina and Honolulu in the Sandwich Islands became important whaling ports. In 1846 almost 600 U.S. whaling ships moored in Hawaii's bays. European and American merchants lobbied their diplomats and naval authorities to activate centuries-old claims on strategic islands so they could annex them as refueling stations and trading centers.

The impact of increased shipping traffic on the native peoples of the Pacific was pronounced. With no immunity to Western illnesses like smallpox, influenza, and syphilis, islanders experienced a holocaust of disease. Little more than a century after the arrival of the *Resolution* and the *Discovery* in Kealakekua Bay, 90 percent of native Hawaiians had perished. Whaling ports in the Pacific became notorious dens of crime and vice. Herman Melville, whose novels educated American readers about the Pacific, was no romantic when he wrote his introduction to *Omoo: A Narrative of Adventures in the South Seas:* "Alas for the savages when exposed to the influence of polluting examples . . . humanity weeps over the ruin inflicted upon them by their European 'civilizers.'"

Missionaries arrived in the Pacific in the late 18th century, often on the same ships whose sailors brought the vice and disease that the missionaries fought. Missionaries intended not only to Christianize islanders but also to westernize them. Bringing farming implements, printing presses, and pump organs along with their Bibles, missionaries wrought more cultural change than any other visitors to the Pacific. Dancing, drums, singing, kava drinking, and tattooing were

Whaling

The Pacific was exploited for all sorts of natural resources in the 19th century, with dire ecological consequences. Sandalwood was harvested on the Fijian, Marquesan, and Hawaiian islands until their forests were depleted. In the first years of the 19th century, more than 300,000 sealskins were sold annually in the trading houses of Canton, China. Seal oil lubricated the machines of early factories in New England and fueled lamps all over the world. Seals became so scarce that in 1819 only 30,000 pelts were traded for the tea, porcelains, and opium desired by American and European consumers.

Even more lucrative than the seal trade, commercial whaling in the Pacific began in the 1790s, reaching its height in the 1840s. Between 1835 and 1855, 722 of the 900 ships whaling in the Pacific were American, many sailing out of Nantucket, Massachusetts, on trips lasting three years or more. Whale oil replaced seal oil as lamp fuel and lubrication. Whalebone from baleen whales provided the raw material for products ranging from umbrella ribs to women's corset stays. Ambergris from the sperm whale was used in making fine perfumes. Sailors on whalers often occupied themselves by etching scenes of whaling or Pacific islands on whale teeth, selling these scrimshaw works in port and bringing them home to New England as souvenirs.

banned by missionaries. Russian explorer Otto von Kotzebue visited Tahiti in 1816 and lamented, "it is a shame that every pleasure should be punished as a sin, especially among a people whom Nature endowed with such a capacity for enjoyment."

Many missionaries had grown up hearing vivid tales of cannibalism, human sacrifice, and infanticide and imagined these rare practices were rampant and needed to be abolished, by force if necessary. More damaging was the missionaries' view of the sexual attitudes and gender roles of the islanders. Islanders had their own distinct cultural beliefs about sexuality that the missionaries could not understand. Seeing sinful behavior where the Pacific peoples saw open and healthy affection, missionaries instituted segregation of the sexes and public shaming. On Tahiti, *mahu*, transgendered people, were honored. In 1798, when a *mahu* desired to become a Christian, one of the ministers sent by the London Missionary Society refused to baptize her.

THE FATEFUL VOYAGE OF LA PÉROUSE

By 1785, Louis XVI was intent on restoring the fortunes of France, both economically and culturally. Its revenues from the North American fur trade were dwindling as trappers depleted the beaver populations of Canada and Louisiana. French colonies in the Caribbean experienced spasms of violence as slaves fought to achieve emancipation. French science remained a point of pride. The Institut National and the Société d'Histoire Naturelle encouraged research and publication in botany, zoology, mathematics, astronomy, and physics. Science and commerce joined together to support France's effort to reassert itself as a colonial power and pro-

pelled the expeditions that followed Louis-Antoine de Bougainville.

In 1785 the French navy fitted two frigates, the *Astrolabe* and the *Boussoule,* for a voyage to the Pacific. Under the command of Jean-François de Galaup, comte de La Pérouse, the expedition brought to the Pacific the largest yet contingent of scientists. La Pérouse's scientific staff included several botanists to study plants, physicists and astronomers to observe the motions of the Earth and heavens, a hyrodrographer to survey coastlines, a mineralologist to examine rock and soil samples, and a natural philosopher to make sense of it all. Attached to the scientific team were draughtsmen to draw maps, an artist charged by La

Jean-François de Galaup, comte de La Pérouse, led an expedition consisting of two ships and many scientists on an extensive journey through the Pacific Ocean that began in 1785 and disappeared in 1788. *(Library of Congress, Prints and Photographs Division [LC-USZ62-78225])*

Paul Gauguin and Robert Louis Stevenson in the South Seas

In 1888, Scottish writer Robert Louis Stevenson (1850–94) was one of the most popular writers in the world. His novels—among them *Dr. Jekyll and Mr. Hyde,* *Treasure Island,* and *Kidnapped*—had made him rich, and Stevenson used his wealth to take his family on a sailing voyage around the South Pacific. In 1889 the Stevenson family arrived in Apia, Samoa, and made it their home. Stevenson intended to write a lengthy anthropological and historical work about the Pacific, and he learned the local dialect well enough to be accepted by the Samoan people, who called him Tusitala—the Teller of Tales. Stevenson never completed his planned work but much of his research was used in *South Sea Tales,* which was published in 1896. He also translated one of his stories, "The Bottle Lamp," into Samoan. Although a foreigner himself, Stevenson joined Samoan leaders in opposing German efforts to colonize Samoa. Stevenson was buried on a mountainside above Apia with honors from his Samoan friends in 1894.

Like Stevenson, the French postimpressionist painter Paul Gauguin (1848–1903) saw the South Pacific both as an escape from the industrialized and commercialized middle-class world of 19th-century Europe. Arriving in Tahiti in 1891, Gauguin wrote, "All the joys—animal and human—of a free life are mine. I have escaped all that is artificial, conventional, customary. I am entering into the truth, into nature."

Also like Stevenson, Gauguin found inspiration for his art in the South Seas. His paintings, which he sent from Tahiti to his dealer in Paris, continue to appeal to viewers with their haunting capture of the natural and the supernatural, the native and the formal. Gauguin left Tahiti in 1901, searching for an evermore "primitive" and unspoiled paradise. He died in the Marquesas in 1903.

Pérouse with "painting dresses and landscapes of the different countries we might visit," a watchmaker to maintain the six chronometers, and a gardener to care for plant specimens.

The *Astrolabe* and the *Boussoule* left Brest, in northwest France, on August 1, 1785. Rounding Cape Horn, the ships visited Easter Island and Hawaii. In late June 1786, La Pérouse brought the ships into an Alaskan harbor he christened Port des Français, now called Lituya Bay. The French traded for furs with Inuit trappers who had, one of La

Pérouse's officers wrote, "manners which were in general more gentle and grave—and who perhaps had greater intelligence than that to be found in any European nation." La Pérouse left Alaska and sailed down the western coast of North America to the Spanish port at Monterey, California. From California the expedition sailed west across the Pacific, touching land in the Hawaiian islands and in the Marianas. The *Astrolabe* and the *Boussoule* entered the Portuguese trading port at Macao, China. The furs from Alaska were sold to brokers in Macao, and one of the scientists returned to

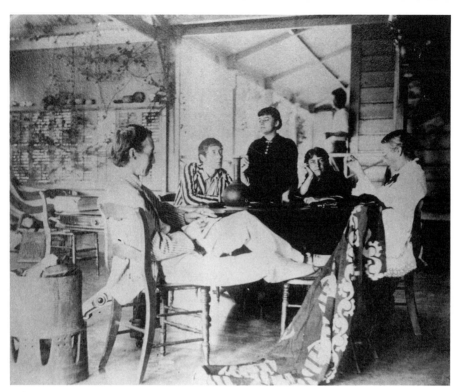

Robert Louis Stevenson used the money he earned from his popular novels to travel around the South Pacific with his family. Stevenson, far left, and family relax in Hawaii. *(Library of Congress, Prints and Photographs Division [LC-USZ62-104639])*

France to deliver the journals and charts generated in the first phase of the expedition.

The expedition left Macao to survey the coasts of China, Korea, and Japan. Returning north in September 1787, La Pérouse arrived at the Russian harbor of Petropavlovsk, where Charles Clerke had died eight years before. Another package of letters, journals, and maps was sent to Paris, and orders from France were waiting for La Pérouse. French officials were concerned about reports that Great Britain was planning a colony at Botany Bay in New Holland. The expedition was to go

there at once to determine the scope of the rivals' new colonial enterprise. Sailing as quickly as possible, stopping only briefly in Samoa and Tonga, the *Astrolabe* and the *Boussoule* reached Botany Bay on January 26, 1788. Despite tensions back in Europe, the governor of New South Wales, Arthur Phillips, received La Pérouse and his officers warmly and offered to convey a shipment of the expedition's documents to France.

In this shipment was a letter from La Pérouse informing the French government of his plans for the next leg of the voyage. He would take his ships to Tonga, then to the Solomons and New Guinea, and return to New Holland to survey its coasts. The French should expect to see the *Astrolabe* and the *Boussoule* in Brest in early December. The ships never returned.

The French Revolution began in 1789. Even in its midst, Louis XVI sent an expedition to find La Pérouse and his ships. The 1791–95 expedition led by Antoine-Raymond-Joseph de Bruni d'Entrecasteaux was equipped as a scientific voyage as well as a rescue effort. The names of d'Entrecasteaux's two ships, *Re-cherche* (research) and *Espérance* (hope), reflect the two purposes of the voyage. Searching widely in the southern Pacific—from Australia, to Van Diemen's Land, to New Zealand, to New Caledonia, and through the Solomons—d'Entrecasteaux's expedition more than fulfilled the scientific aspects of its assignment. But no sign of La Pérouse was found. The aftermath of the revolution and the wars of Napoleon Bonaparte would draw French attention away from the Pacific. Between 1800 and 1803, the *Géographe* and the *Naturaliste*, under the command of Nicholas-Thomas

George Vancouver explored a large island off the western coast of North America that would later be named for him—Vancouver Island—in the early 1790s. This watercolor by J. Ross dates from that time. *(National Archives of Canada)*

Baudin, collected 100,000 botanic and zoological specimens from New Zealand and Van Diemen's Land. This was the last French expedition sent to the Pacific until 1817.

THE BRITISH SURVEYORS

Even though James Cook had not located the Northwest Passage on his third voyage, Britain's interest in the passage was undiminished. In 1791 the Admiralty sent George Vancouver, a veteran of Cook's second and third voyages, in search of both the passage and

greater knowledge of the natural history of the northern Pacific. The Admiralty also wanted intelligence about the activities of Spanish explorers and traders in the region. Many of Cook's officers and sailors joined the crews of the *Chatham* and a new ship christened *Discovery* in honor of Captain Cook. Archibald Menzies served as the expedition naturalist. Astronomer William Gooch was sent to meet the ships in the Sandwich Islands but died before he could join Vancouver. Kualelo, a man from Molokai who had come to England on the first *Discovery,* traveled back to Hawaii with Vancouver.

Departing from Falmouth in April, Vancouver took the expedition around the Cape of Good Hope and then to New Holland. Pausing at Van Diemen's Land, the *Chatham* and the *Discovery* made for New Zealand's Dusky Bay. From New Zealand, Vancouver sailed to Tahiti, where the ships spent three weeks taking on provisions. On March 3, 1792, the *Chatham* and the *Discovery* anchored in Kealakekua Bay. Much had changed since Vancouver had been there three years before. Several American and European ships had visited the islands, and two Americans were living on Hawaii. Vancouver reported that he met a man named Kaiana who had traveled to China on a fur-trading ship. King Kamehameha ruled all of Hawaii, unifying islands that had previously been linked only by kinship and trade and governed by local chiefs.

Vancouver stayed in the Sandwich Islands just long enough to prepare his ships for six weeks at sea en route to California. His orders were to explore the Pacific coast from 30° to 60° north latitude to find the Northwest Passage, or any other large rivers that would encourage settlement, and therefore trade, in western Canada. Reaching the California coast about 120 miles north of San Francisco, the *Chatham* and the *Discovery* sailed north along the coast. Vancouver heard from U.S. fur trader Robert Gray about a great river Gray had named after his ship, the *Columbia.* After difficulty finding the mouth of the Columbia, Vancouver sent a small boat 100 miles up the river to explore. The *Chatham* and the *Discovery* entered the Strait of Juan de Fuca in late April 1792. Vancouver anchored in a bay he named Discovery and established a camp onshore. For six weeks this camp housed the expedition while the ships were overhauled, functioned as a laboratory and observatory for scientists, and served as a base for exploration of the region. Boats sent south charted a sound Vancouver named after his second lieutenant, Peter Puget. Surveyors sent north determined that a large landmass, now named Vancouver Island, on the west coast of the strait was not attached to the mainland.

The expedition spent the winter of 1792–93 in Hawaii and returned to Nootka Sound in May 1793 to survey regions north and south of the sound. The *Chatham* and the *Discovery,* joined by the supply ship *Daedelus,* spent fall 1793 surveying the coast of California as far south as Baja California. This was Spain's territory, and Vancouver was not welcomed, either as an officer of the Royal Navy or as a geographer. Returning to Hawaii for the winter, Vancouver was convinced of the islands' value as a way station for British ships in the Pacific. He persuaded Kamehameha that a benevolent England would protect Hawaii from the designs of the Americans and the Spanish. On February 25, 1794, Kamehameha ceded the Hawaiian islands to Great Britain, but the British Parliament never ratified the cession.

The Vancouver expedition returned to American shores a third time in April to complete its survey to the prescribed 60° north latitude. Landing at Kodiak Island, Vancouver conducted a complete survey of Cook Inlet and confirmed Cook's finding that the inlet was not the Northwest Passage. The last part of Vancouver's survey took the ships to 56° north latitude to a cove on Baranof Island he named Port Conclusion. During the many months Vancouver had spent in the northwest Pacific, he had encountered many Spanish traders and some Spanish naval ships. By the time Vancouver returned to England in October 1795 and made his report about the Spanish presence, Great Britain and Spain had reached an agreement that kept Nootka Sound open to traders from both nations. Home in England, Vancouver prepared *A Voyage of Discovery in the North Pacific Ocean and Round the World.* Its three volumes and atlas document his spectacular achievements. Vancouver had completed a survey of the Pacific coast of America, made the first complete charts of the Hawaiian islands, and proved that—if it existed at all—the Northwest Passage would be found above the Bering Strait.

An English naval officer stationed in Botany Bay, Matthew Flinders, said he was inspired to go to sea after reading the novel *Robinson Crusoe.* In 1791 he had sailed in the Pacific with William Bligh on a second expedition to import breadfruit trees to Britain's colonies in the Caribbean. In 1795 he was sent to New South Wales with John Hunter, the colony's new governor. From Botany Bay, Flinders made many short trips to explore the south coast of New Holland in a little boat he named the *Tom Thumb.* An amateur explorer, George Bass, reported in 1797 that he was sure that Tasmania was separated from New Holland by a strait. Governor Hunter commissioned Flinders to sail the *Norfolk* to confirm the report and conduct "such examinations and surveys on the way as circumstances might permit." Flinders completed a survey of the strait, returned to England in 1800, and published his findings. He dedicated his book to Joseph Banks, the gentleman botanist of the *Endeavour*.

Banks had by then become president of the Royal Society and Flinders petitioned him to support an exploration of the coast of New Holland. Banks recommended the mission to the Admiralty, and the *Investigator* was prepared for the voyage. The Admiralty knew of Nicholas-Thomas Baudin's expedition and was anxious to secure Tasmania under the flag of Great Britain. The *Investigator* sailed for New Holland on July 18, 1801, with a staff of scientists on board. The Royal Botanic Gardens at Kew, outside London, had become a gallery for plant specimens gathered during British expeditions, and gardener Peter Good sailed on the *Investigator* to collect plants for Kew. A mining expert also accompanied the expedition to determine if New Holland would ever become a profitable possession for Great Britain. Flinders arrived in New Holland in early December and spent the next year surveying the coast of New Holland, completing the first circumnavigation of the continent. Britain was once again at war with France in fall 1803 as Flinders sailed for the Cape of Good Hope. Flinders was shipwrecked near the Torres Strait and then captured by the French in the Indian Ocean. Imprisoned as a spy on Mauritius for more than six years, Flinders did not see England until October 1810. He published *A Voyage to Terra Australis* shortly before he died. In it, Flinders was the first to call the continent of New Holland "Australia."

MEN OF SCIENCE

Napoleon Bonaparte's wars with Great Britain, Spain, Austria, and Russia drained France's treasury until 1815, when French troops were defeated at Waterloo, Belgium. In 1817, with the French monarchy restored and Louis XVIII on the throne, France turned its attention once more to the Pacific. Louis-Claude-Desaules de Freycinet commanded the *Uranie* during its three-year circumnavigation, an expedition intended to make astronomical observations from Australia and New Guinea. The cartographer of the *Uranie*, Louis-Isidore Duperrey, felt that Freycinet had neglected the scientific work of his expedition. In 1822 he was given command of the *Coquille* for a scientific expedition to the Pacific. The *Coquille* sailed widely, visiting the Tuamotus, Tahiti, Bora Bora, the Solomons, New Ireland, Australia, the Carolines, New Guinea, and Java. But the three-year expedition contributed little to the fields of botany and zoology, and nothing to cartography because Duperrey's charts were poorly made.

Jules-Sébastien-César Dumont d'Urville had been second-in-command on the *Coquille*. Dumont d'Urville wanted to return to the southern Pacific to accurately chart the discoveries made by previous French expeditions, as Vancouver had done after Cook's surveys in the northern Pacific. He also wanted to go farther, to restore the French to their position as preeminent explorers. Finally, his expedition would search for clues about the fate of La Pérouse. The *Coquille* was prepared for the voyage, and Dumont d'Urville asked it be renamed the *Astrolabe*, in honor of La Pérouse. The *Astrolabe* sailed from Toulon in southern France in April 1826. Its 34-month voyage took it to Australia, New Zealand, Tonga, Fiji, the Moluccas, and New Guinea. On Vanikoro in the Santa Cruz islands, Dumont d'Urville was given or purchased guns, cooking pots, and navigational instruments of French manufacture and accepted the relics as proof that La Pérouse had lost his ship near the island.

The scientists and artists of the *Astrolabe* produced 6,000 drawings and conducted enough research to fill 14 volumes of botany, zoology, and ethnography. Dumont d'Urville himself became something of an ethnographer, noting the distinctions between the peoples of the regions he visited and classifying them as Melanesian, Micronesian, and Polynesian. He speculated that the Papua people of New Guinea might be descended from the ancient Egyptians, because their jewelry and raised tombs looked like artifacts that French soldiers had brought from Egypt after Napoleon's campaign in 1799. Dumont d'Urville returned to a France in turmoil. King Charles V was forced from his throne in 1830, and Dumont d'Urville was assigned to escort him into exile.

In December 1831, Robert FitzRoy set off from England on a surveying mission on the *Beagle.* His ship carried 22 chronometers, an experiment to determine which model kept time, and therefore determined longitude, most accurately. The ship also carried a 22-year-old naturalist, Charles Darwin. Darwin's role was to collect specimens and record his observations about weather, geology, plants, animals, fossils, and native peoples. For two years the *Beagle* surveyed the east coast of South America. Traversing the Strait of Magellan, the *Beagle* entered the Pacific in spring 1834 and headed for Callao, in Peru. Darwin spent almost a year in Peru and Chile collecting specimens and studying the geology of the Andes. In February 1835, the *Beagle* sailed to a group of islands known as Los Encantados, 620 miles west of Ecuador. Of these islands, now called the Galapagos, Darwin observed, "the natural history of this archipelago is very remarkable, it seems to be a little world within itself." Darwin noticed that the animals on the Galapagos resembled those of South America and that the fossils of extinct species he found bore many similarities to living animals but were not identical.

Charles Darwin's five-year voyage as a naturalist aboard the *Beagle* helped him generate revolutionary ideas about species and their development. *(Library of Congress, Prints and Photographs Division [LC-USZ61-104])*

As the *Beagle* sailed through the Pacific over the next year, Darwin continued to develop his theory that species changed over long periods of time. The *Beagle* visited Tahiti, New Zealand, Tasmania, and Australia. Darwin closely studied the large and small islands that passed. He created a classification system for coral reefs that is still used today, distinguishing among fringe reefs, barrier reefs, and atolls. Darwin also theorized that many of the islands he saw were the remnants of eroded volcanoes. When the *Beagle* returned to England, he published his work on reef formation, *The Structure and Distribution of Coral Reefs.* The most significant result of Darwin's four

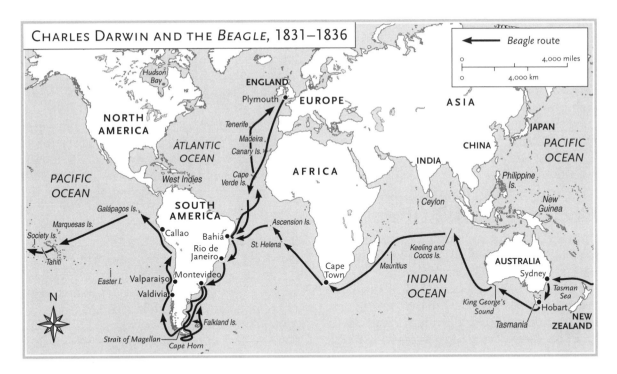

CHARLES DARWIN AND THE *BEAGLE*, 1831–1836

Beagle route

4,000 miles
4,000 km

Hudson Bay

NORTH AMERICA

ATLANTIC OCEAN

West Indies

PACIFIC OCEAN

Galápagos Is.

Marquesas Is.

Society Is.

Tahiti

Easter I.

Callao

Valparaiso

Valdivia

Montevideo

SOUTH AMERICA

Bahia

Rio de Janeiro

Falkland Is.

Strait of Magellan

Cape Horn

N

ENGLAND

Plymouth

EUROPE

Tenerife

Madeira

Canary Is.

Cape Verde Is.

AFRICA

Ascension Is.

St. Helena

Cape Town

ASIA

CHINA

JAPAN

INDIA

PACIFIC OCEAN

Ceylon

Philippine Is.

New Guinea

INDIAN OCEAN

Mauritius

Keeling and Cocos Is.

King George's Sound

AUSTRALIA

Sydney

Tasman Sea

Hobart

NEW ZEALAND

Tasmania

Visited by Charles Darwin and the *Beagle*, the Galápagos Islands are shown covered in iguanas in this early 1900s photograph. *(Library of Congress, Prints and Photographs Division [LC-USZ62-105188])*

and a half years on the *Beagle* was his book *On the Origin of Species by Means of Natural Selection.* His observations on a small Pacific archipelago led Darwin to write a book that challenged traditional ideas about the creation of life, a book that started a revolution in science by setting forth early ideas of evolution.

FARTHER THAN COOK

Dumont d'Urville, still hoping to raise France to the highest rank of achievement in exploration, proposed another expedition for the *Astrolabe* in 1837. Accompanied by the *Zelée,* the *Astrolabe* sailed to Tierra del Fuego, arriving in January 1838. The new king, Louis-Philippe, had commanded Dumont d'Urville to drive his ships farther south in the Antarctic Circle than Cook had ever sailed. Dumont d'Urville acknowledged his king's desire to best the British, but his own purpose in voyaging south was to calculate the position of the magnetic South Pole. Expedition scientists carried out the first study and classification of polar marine life as the ships sailed toward Antarctica. At 65° south latitude, the ice became impossible to penetrate. Dumont d'Urville wrote in his *Voyage au Pôle Sud et dans L'Océanie* about the awesome sight of an endless field of immense ice blocks jumbled on top of one another. "It was indeed a new world that unfolded ahead of us, but a world that was colorless, silent and the very negation of life."

Like Cook before him, Dumont d'Urville made a forced retreat to warmer latitudes. The *Astrolabe* and the *Zelée* became trapped in ice three times in February, and their crews were sick with scurvy. Dumont d'Urville turned his ships toward Chile and rested his men at Talcahuano for six weeks. The expedition spent 18 months in the southern Pacific before returning to the Antarctic Circle. Its scientists collected a wide array of zoological specimens, from an albatross to a Tasmanian devil. Heading first to the Marquesas, Dumont d'Urville sailed his ships to Tahiti, Tonga, and the Solomons. The *Astrolabe* and the *Zelée* cruised through the Philippines, explored the length of New Guinea, sailed all the way around Borneo, and arrived in Hobart, Tasmania, in December 1839.

The next month, January 1840, Dumont d'Urville led his ships south once again. On January 19, they sailed into the Antarctic Circle. At 66°30' south latitude, great cliffs of ice appeared along a shoreline that seemed without end. Dumont d'Urville checked his compasses. Their needles whipped back and forth. No two gave the same reading. He knew that at last Terra Australis Incognita had been found. Three days later the *Astrolabe's* boat carried Dumont d'Urville to the shore of a rocky island just a few hundred feet from the mainland. He planted the French flag, toasted his discovery with a glass of Bordeaux, and claimed the southern continent for France. As the *Astrolabe* and the *Zelée* made their precarious way north through the ice, enduring blizzards and gale force winds, Dumont d'Urville saw another ship. From its mast flew the flag of the United States. With unbelieving eyes, Dumont d'Urville watched the ship change course and sail out of sight into the sleet and fog.

THE UNITED STATES EXPLORING EXPEDITION AND THE *CHALLENGER*

Dumont d'Urville had seen the *Porpoise,* a ship of the United States Exploring Expedition. In 1838, Congress appropriated $300,000 to the navy for a "surveying and exploring

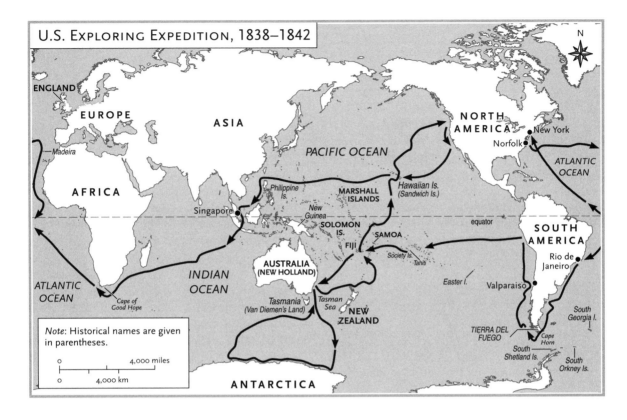

U.S. EXPLORING EXPEDITION, 1838–1842

Note: Historical names are given in parentheses.

expedition to the Pacific Ocean and South Seas." One purpose of the expedition was to create accurate charts and maps for the ships that were sailing farther south and west in search of increasingly scarce whales. Without such charts whaling captains sailed blind, with no knowledge of islands, currents, or weather patterns. Shipwrecked sailors could be drowned, marooned on desolate islands, or, worst of all, washed up in Japan, where U.S. sailors were imprisoned as criminals. The commander of what came to be known as "the Endless Expedition" was Lieutenant Charles Wilkes. Along with the *Vincennes,* five other ships were assigned to the expedition: the *Peacock,* the *Relief,* the *Porpoise,* the *Seagull,* and the *Flying Fish.* Three hundred and forty-two sailors, 89 officers, nine scientists, and the

artist Titian Ramsey Peale made up the company of the expedition. The ships left Norfolk, Virginia, on August 18, 1838.

When the fleet reached Tierra del Fuego in mid-August, Wilkes, who had promoted himself to the rank of captain, directed his ships to separate. Wilkes would sail on the *Porpoise* and, accompanied by the *Seagull,* would go to the South Shetland and South Orkney islands. The *Peacock* and the *Flying Fish* would explore to the southwest. The *Vincennes* and the *Relief* would survey Tierra del Fuego and the Strait of Magellan. When the ships rendezvoused in Valparaiso, Chile, in April 1839, the *Seagull* failed to appear. No trace of the ship was ever found. From Valparaiso the expedition sailed west into the Pacific and spent the summer months surveying its islands. Wilkes oversaw the first survey of the Tuamotu group, documenting two previously unknown islands. The expedition called at Tahiti, Samoa, and the Marshall Islands before reaching Australia in December.

Wilkes launched his second Antarctic attempt from Australia in January 1840. A sailor caught an emperor penguin as the expedition sailed south. When the biologists examined its stomach contents, they found small pebbles and knew they were nearing land. Wilkes, whose dictatorial manner may have been the inspiration for *Moby Dick*'s Captain Ahab, was determined to be the first man to

see Antarctica. His log states that he did so on January 11, but evidence suggests that Wilkes altered the log. As the climate turned frigid, the expedition surgeons presented a formal statement that they believed sailors would begin to die if the ships sailed any farther south into the Antarctic Circle. Many of the officers supported the surgeons, but Wilkes refused to sail to lower latitudes. Sailors on the *Flying Fish* petitioned their captain to turn around, and he took the ship to New Zealand. On January 30 the *Porpoise* came within shouting distance of Dumont d'Urville's ships but veered away without acknowledging the French vessels.

Just as the members of the expedition were contemplating mutiny, Wilkes took the ships north to Australia. The so-called Endless Expedition completed the first thorough surveys of Tahiti and the Samoan and Hawaiian islands, and then sailed to the coast of North America. Much of 1841 was occupied in surveying the northwest coast of the continent. Wilkes wrote a memo arguing that the United States should insist on setting its border with Canada at 54°40' north latitude. This would assure the United States of excellent deepwater ports from which U.S. shipping could dominate trade in the Pacific. As if to demonstrate the soundness of this argument, the United States Exploring Expedition set sail for the Philippines.

Wilkes negotiated a trading agreement with the sultan of Sulu, an island group at the southern tip of the Philippines. On the way to the Cape of Good Hope, the expedition called at Singapore, just south of Malacca. Like Alfonso de Albuquerque three centuries before, Wilkes sought trading opportunities on Malay Peninsula to increase his nation's wealth. The United States Exploring Expedition entered New York harbor in July 1842. The hydrographers, geographers, and draughts-

Charles Wilkes commanded an expedition of five ships whose purpose was to chart and survey the Pacific Ocean. *(Library of Congress, Prints and Photographs Division [LC-B8172-1371])*

men of the expedition had hundreds of charts and maps ready to be printed. James Dwight Dana, an expedition scientist, would join Darwin's scientific revolution with the research he had carried out during the Endless Expedition. Thousands of specimens and artifacts were crated for shipment to the new Smithsonian Institution. But 23 men had lost their lives on the voyage, more than 100 sailors had deserted, and three ships were lost or destroyed. Wilkes was brought before a court-martial on several charges. He was found guilty of illegally punishing his seamen. It was never proved to the court's satisfaction that Wilkes had altered the *Porpoise*'s log to support his claims of discovering Antarctica.

The last great 19th-century expedition to the Pacific introduced an entirely new form of exploration and pioneered a new science, oceanography. Led by Sir Wyville Thompson, the *Challenger* expedition spent the years from 1873–76 systematically studying 68,890 nautical miles of ocean from the north Atlantic, through the Pacific, to the Antarctic Circle. The *Challenger* was a 226-foot-long, three-masted warship specifically modified for the expedition. Its guns were removed to make room for laboratories, workrooms, and storage for specimens. A 1,200-horsepower stream engine was installed so the ship could trawl for specimens at a steady speed and maneuver close to shore. One hundred and forty-four miles of hemp rope and twelve and a half miles of piano wire were provided to lower specimen-collecting jars to the ocean floor. A hundred scientists carried out experiments.

The chief scientists selected 362 stations, located at uniform distances from one another. Moving from station to station, the *Challenger* measured the depth of the ocean, the temperature at the bottom, temperatures at various depths, and the strength and direction of the current. Scientists collected samples of the ocean floor, water, plants, and marine animals at each station. Naturalist Henry Mosely recalled that "when the dredge came up every man and boy who could possibly slip away crowded 'round it." The samples were carefully cataloged and stored in special cases made to withstand the pitch and roll of the ship in rough seas.

When the *Challenger* returned to England, the scope of its achievements was awesome. Its discoveries still guide oceanographic research in the Pacific. The *Challenger* expedition developed the first plot of the currents of the Pacific. Its scientists created the first outline of the main contours of the ocean basins. It measured the greatest Pacific depth then known, the Challenger Deep. During the expedition, 4,717 new species were discovered and classified. And where the ocean depths had been thought to be cold, dark, dead zones, the floating laboratories of the *Challenger* proved that life flourishes even in the deepest reaches of the Pacific.

SEA POWER

In the 1880s, a 45-year-old officer in the U.S. Navy entertained himself in his off-duty hours reading Roman history. Alfred Thayer Mahan became persuaded that the Roman Empire had come to dominate much of the known world on the strength of its naval forces. Mahan debuted this theory in a paper given at the Naval War College and expanded his argument in *The Influence of Sea Power upon History, 1660–1783*, published in 1890. Mahan's influence on the great powers—the United States, France, Germany, and Great Britain—was immense. Mahan wrote that a large, well-armed navy was essential to protect trade and would guarantee national wealth and international influence. Eleven nations had larger navies than the United States in 1880. By 1900 the U.S. Navy was the third largest in the world.

European countries had long used their navies to protect merchant ships, and the United States was no stranger to doing so. In 1818 the frigate *Constitution* was sent to protect U.S. ships in the Pacific. Naval stations had been established at Valparaiso, Chile, and Callao, Peru, in the 1820s to support a fledgling Pacific fleet. When the merchant ship *Friendship* was attacked in Sumatra in 1832, President Andrew Jackson sent the *USS Potomac* to demand restitution. Commodore Matthew Perry sailed a fleet of nine warships the Japanese called *kurofune* ("black, evil-looking boats") into Tokyo Bay in 1853. Eighteen hundred sailors and more than 140 guns forced the Japanese into opening their ports to U.S. ships. In 1878, Ulysses S. Grant had made a treaty with Samoan leaders to establish a naval station at Pago Pago.

Motivated by *The Influence of Sea Power upon History*, Massachusetts senator Henry Cabot Lodge argued before the Senate, "Sea power consists in the first place of a proper navy and a proper fleet, but in order to sustain a navy, we must have suitable ports for naval stations." The islands of the Pacific that had served as coaling stations and whaling ports were now seen as strategic naval bases. Mahan published an article in 1893 recommending Hawaii, "as a position powerfully influencing the commercial and military control of the Pacific, and especially of the Northern Pacific in which the United States, geographically, has the strongest right to assert herself." The United States annexed Hawaii in 1898 and built its largest naval base at Pearl Harbor.

That same year, in the four-month-long Spanish-American War, Commodore George Dewey directed the U.S. Pacific Fleet to victory over Spanish forces in Manila Bay, the Philippines. Annexation of the Philippines and Guam was hotly debated in the United States. Novelist and humorist Mark Twain called the supporters of a U.S. Pacific empire the "Blessings of Civilization Trust" and warned, "We are destroying the lives of these islanders." Whitelaw Reid, the influential editor of New York's *Herald-Tribune*, argued for empire. The United States, Reid demanded, must seize the opportunity to "convert the Pacific Ocean into an American lake." Under the terms of the 1899 Treaty of Paris, the United States did annex the Philippines and Guam. Naval bases were quickly established at Cavite in Manila Bay and Apra Harbor on Guam.

By the end of the 19th century, the United States and the nations of Europe controlled the destiny of the Pacific. Spain, utterly defeated by its loss of the Philippines, sold the Mariana, Marshall, and Caroline Islands to Germany. Germany also had possessions in Samoa and the Solomons. France maintained sovereignty over Tahiti, the Marquesas, and many small island groups in Polynesia. The Dutch retained some presence in the region, claiming parts of New Guinea and sharing sovereignty over Timor with their old rival Portugal. Great Britain shared control of the New Hebrides with France, and of the Solomons with Germany. Britain's great ports in Hong Kong and Singapore serviced a Pacific fleet that protected British possessions in Papua New Guinea, Fiji, and the Gilbert and Ellice islands.

World War II would prove Alfred Thayer Mahan right. On December 7, 1941, Japanese planes attacked the U.S. naval base at Pearl Harbor. On the same day and at the same time, Japan destroyed almost all of U.S. Pacific airpower by bombing hundreds of planes on the ground at the Clark army air force base near Manila. Japan had gained the Marshall,

Commodore George Dewey led the U.S. Pacific Fleet to victory over Spanish forces at the Battle of Manila Bay during the Spanish-American War. *(Library of Congress, Prints and Photographs Division [LC-B8172-105269])*

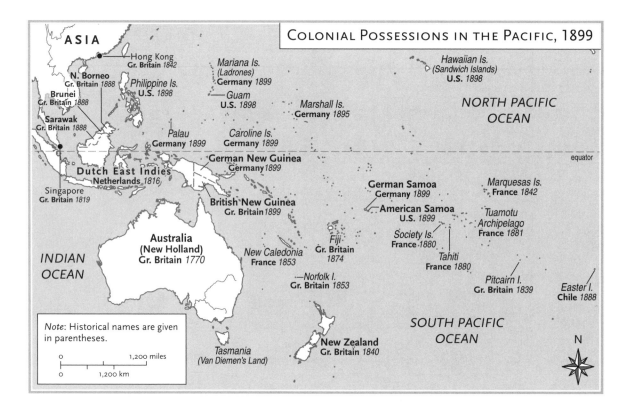

COLONIAL POSSESSIONS IN THE PACIFIC, 1899

ASIA

Hong Kong
Gr. Britain 1842

N. Borneo
Gr. Britain 1888

Philippine Is.
U.S. 1898

Brunei
Gr. Britain 1888

Sarawak
Gr. Britain 1888

Mariana Is.
(Ladrones)
Germany 1899

Guam
U.S. 1898

Palau
Germany 1899

Caroline Is.
Germany 1899

Marshall Is.
Germany 1895

Hawaiian Is.
(Sandwich Islands)
U.S. 1898

NORTH PACIFIC
OCEAN

Dutch East Indies
Netherlands 1816

Singapore
Gr. Britain 1819

German New Guinea
Germany 1899

equator

British New Guinea
Gr. Britain 1899

German Samoa
Germany 1899

American Samoa
U.S. 1899

Marquesas Is.
France 1842

Tuamotu
Archipelago
France 1881

INDIAN
OCEAN

Australia
(New Holland)
Gr. Britain 1770

New Caledonia
France 1853

Fiji
Gr. Britain
1874

Society Is.
France 1880

Tahiti
France 1880

Pitcairn I.
Gr. Britain 1839

Easter I.
Chile 1888

Norfolk I.
Gr. Britain 1853

SOUTH PACIFIC
OCEAN

N

Note: Historical names are given
in parentheses.

0   1,200 miles

0   1,200 km

Tasmania
(Van Diemen's Land)

New Zealand
Gr. Britain 1840

Caroline, and Mariana Islands in the aftermath of Germany's defeat in World War I. Japanese forces moved south from these islands to vanquish U.S. forces from the Philippines in May 1942. The loss of the Philippines was a terrible blow to allied efforts in the Pacific. Earlier that year, the British Royal Navy had lost its largest Pacific port when Singapore fell to Japan in February. With Singapore and the Philippines in Japanese hands, U.S. and Allied ships relied on the strategic ports claimed in the last years of the 19th century. Great fleets of battleships and aircraft carriers sailed from Espíritu Santo, Pearl Harbor, and New Caledonia. From Atuk and Kiska in the Aleutian Islands to the Solomons, war raged throughout the Pacific, including in Wake Island, Guadalcanal, and the Coral Sea. Where Álvaro de Mendaña de Neyra, Willem Janz, James Cook, and Charles Wilkes had explored in the service of God, in the service of trade, in the service of empire, and in the service of science, the waters of the Pacific were washed with blood.

GLOSSARY

Admiralty The department of the British government assigned responsibility for the administration of all naval affairs, including managing personnel, building and supplying ships, conducting naval expeditions, and regulating maritime law.

aft A position near or at the stern, or rear, of a ship.

ambergris An ash-colored substance secreted in the intestines of the sperm whale. It was used to fix the fragrance of fine perfumes in the 19th century and was a principal product of the whaling industry.

antiscorbutic Food or medicine that prevents scurvy.

armada A fleet of warships.

asiento An exclusive contract granted by the Spanish Crown from the 16th to late 18th century to private trading companies of friendly nations. An asiento gave the holder a monopoly on trade with a particular Spanish colony. It also stipulated tariffs and duties.

astrolabe An instrument that determines latitude. It measures the height of a heavenly body (the sun or stars). A flat metal ring with a rotating arm, the astrolabe is suspended from the navigator's thumb. The navigator then looks through two pinhole sights on the astrolabe's arm to measure the angle of elevation of the object.

atoll Formed of coral reefs, a circular island enclosing a lagoon.

Austronesian Ancestors of the earliest Pacific people, originating in Asia, and the ancestors of the aboriginal people of Australia. The term also refers to the group of languages spoken in much of the Pacific.

bark A large sailing ship, with three or more square-rigged masts. The aftermost mast is fore- and aft-rigged, with sails hung to its front and back.

breadfruit Starchy round fruit about the size of a grapefruit that was used as a staple food on many Pacific islands at the time of contact with Europeans. Breadfruit trees were imported from the Pacific to the Caribbean by the English as a cheap food source for slaves.

brigantine A nimble sailing ship, originally used as a fighting ship, with two masts. The foremast is square-rigged and the mainmast is fore- and aft-rigged with square upper sails.

caravel A small sailing ship with triangular sails used for coastal exploration by the Portuguese and Spanish in the 15th and 16th centuries.

careening A process involving the emptying of ships and turning them on their sides to replace rotted planks, remove growths of barnacles, and coat the hull with pitch from pine trees to prevent worms from eating the wood.

carrack With its origins in the Mediterranean, the basic form of ship used for ocean-going trading and exploration in the 16th century. Spanish records often refer to a carrack as a *nao*.

cat-o-nine tails A whip made of unraveled hemp rope used in the English navy to punish sailors for shipboard crimes.

court-martial A court procedure that tries military personnel for crimes against military law. The judges are members of the military. The term is also used to refer to a trial held in a court-martial.

cross-staff A simple instrument used to calculate latitude. A three-foot-long stick marked with degrees, with a moveable slat fixed to it, the cross-staff is held to the navigator's eye and the crosspiece slides along the staff until one end is aligned with a celestial body and the other with the horizon.

dead reckoning An elementary form of navigation in which position is calculated by the course and distance traveled from a known point.

dhow A generic term for a small, swift boat with one mast and a lateen (triangular) sail used by Arab traders in the Indian Ocean and along the coast of East Africa.

doldrums Located between 5° north and 5° south of the equator, a band of calm winds and light currents that often stalls sailing ships crossing the Pacific for weeks or months.

duty A tax imposed on goods imported or exported.

entrepot Technically refers to a port at which goods can be imported and exported without duty. Entrepot has come to mean a port or city at which the main commercial activity is importing, storing, trading, and exporting goods.

flotilla A group of small ships or a small group of ships.

fluyt A sturdy ship with an almost flat hull used in the 17th century by the Dutch for trading and exploring.

fore A position at or near the bow, or front, of a ship. The foremast is the mast nearest the bow of a ship.

forecastle Pronounced "foke-sell," the raised part of a ship's deck in front of the foremast. In some ships the forecastle housed the crew's quarters.

fothering An emergency, at-sea repair to a ship's hull involving patching the hole with sailcloth held in place by suction.

frigate Medium-sized warship used mostly between 1750 and 1850. A frigate could carry as many as 50 cannons, which were housed on a separate gun deck as well as on the top deck. They carried three square-rigged masts and were considered very fast ships.

galleon A large sailing ship with three or more masts. With square rigging, the galleon was the principal ship used for ocean voyaging from the 15th to the 18th centuries.

galley The basic form of ship used in the Mediterranean Sea until the 14th century. By the 13th century galleys had sails, although oarsmen could be employed when the winds were low or in rough seas. Italian galleys of the 13th century could be as long as 120 to 150 feet long, carrying a crew of more than 200 men.

gibbet A wooden frame, a gallows, with an extending crossbar. They were used until the 19th century to display the bodies of executed people and served as a warning against criminal actions.

hull The rounded bottom of a ship or boat that is partially underwater. Because it is hollow, the hull helps the vessel float. The shape of the hull can affect the stability and speed of a ship.

jacht A small, light trading vessel with two masts; one of the earliest Dutch ships to sail to the East Indies. The term *yacht* is derived from the word *jacht*.

junk Its name derived from the Chinese word for "river," a large sailing ship developed around A.D. 200. Having two or three masts, junks can be as large as 1,500 tons and can carry up to a thousand crewmembers and passengers.

kava Meaning "bitter" in several Polynesian dialects, it refers both to a pepper plant found throughout the islands of the South Pacific and to the mildly intoxicating drink that is brewed from it. Kava was used as currency between islands until Europeans introduced money and it served a role in some cultures' religious rituals.

latitude The designation of distance from the equator. It is measured in degrees. The North Pole is located at 90° north, the equator at 0°, and the South Pole at 90° south.

longitude The designation of distance east or west of the north-south line, the prime meridian, located at Greenwich, England.

league A common unit of measurement in western Europe, originally referring to the distance a person could walk in an hour. At sea a league is equivalent to three nautical miles (three minutes of latitude), which would be about the same as 3.45 miles on land.

man-o-war A large warship that could carry as many as 100 cannons. Men-o-War carried three square-rigged masts, with a lateen sail on the aft mast. Men-o-war were expensive to build and maintain, and as a result only France, England, and Spain built and used them in the 18th century.

marine chronometer Essentially a clock designed to keep time under the hard conditions at sea. The chronometer was invented in the mid-18th century, perhaps the most important development in the search for an accurate method of determining longitude. The chronometer was first extensively tested on Captain James Cook's second voyage, and he came to call it "our never-failing guide." It has always kept time at the prime meridian, 0° longitude, which had been fixed at Greenwich, England, the site of the Royal Observatory. A navigator would use a sextant to measure the local time, convert the difference, and calculate longitude, multiplying each hour by 15.

marine A soldier serving on a ship. Marines' quarters in the Age of Exploration were generally located between the cabins of the officers and the bunks of the crewmembers. One of their roles was to protect the ship's officers in case of a mutiny. Marines also served as armed protection for parties going ashore when a welcome by area inhabitants was uncertain.

mast An upright pole that holds a ship's rigging and sails.

papal bull A legal opinion delivered by the pope and certified with an official seal. The word *bull* derives from the Latin word for "seal." Before the Reformation, papal bulls were given the weight of international law and recognized as binding by most European nations.

pinnace A small, light boat used as an escort for a larger ship. Pinnaces were often used during the 18th century to explore coastlines and river inlets.

quadrant A simple instrument used to measure latitude. The quadrant consists of a quarter circle of wood or metal, with degree marks along its curved edge. A plumb line hangs from the intersection of the two straight edges, to indicate a vertical position. Sights on one of the straight edges are aligned with the sun or the North Star, and measurements are then taken of distance from the horizon.

rigging The system of ropes, and sometimes chains, that support and move the sails of a ship. The word can also be used to refer to the shape of the sails or design of the sail system. For example, a lateen-rigged ship has triangular sails on an angled yard. A square-rigged ship has square sails.

Royal Observatory Established by English king Charles II at Greenwich, England, in 1675, this organization's primary purpose was to foster study and documentation of astronomical conditions that would lead to a method for calculating longitude at sea. Prizes of up to £20,000 were to be awarded to the most accurate method, and a Board of Longitude was established to supervise testing.

scrimshaw The art of carving or engraving pictures on whales' teeth or whalebone. The word comes from the English navy term *scrimshanker,* which means "time waster." Scrimshaw was a popular hobby for sailors on 19th-century whaling ships in the Pacific, who used lamp soot or squid ink to color the etched designs. Scrimshaw scenes depicted the capture and killing of whales, island paradises, and biblical stories. The teeth were sometimes drilled to make cribbage boards or hollowed to make tobacco containers. Whalebone was carved to fashion umbrella handles or household tools like pie crimpers.

sextant An instrument used to measure the angle of celestial bodies to the horizon. Developed in 1757, the sextant was a great advance because it can measure angles accurate to within one-tenth of a degree. The sextant is a metal curve with two straight edges and small telescope and mirror attached.

skiff A small boat often carried on board large sailing ships to make expeditions to shore.

speculation Usage of some degree of stock market manipulation or insider knowledge in order to reap huge financial gain from a small investment.

strait A passage that connects two larger bodies of water.

tariff A list or schedule of the taxes that must be paid on imported or exported goods.

yard A long pole attached perpendicular or at an angle to a mast and to which sails are attached.

FURTHER INFORMATION

NONFICTION

Alexander, Caroline. "The Wreck of the Pandora," *The New Yorker,* August 4, 2003: 44–59.

Aughton, Peter. *Endeavour: The Story of Captain Cook's First Great Epic Voyage.* Moreton-on-Marsh, England: Windrush Press, 1999.

Badger, Geoffrey. *The Explorers of the Pacific.* Kenthurst, New South Wales: Kangaroo Press, 1996.

Beaglehole, J. C. *The Exploration of the Pacific.* 3rd edition. Stanford: Stanford University Press, 1966.

Bolster, Jeffrey W. *Black Jacks: African-American Seamen in the Age of Sail.* Cambridge, Mass.: Harvard University Press, 1998.

Cameron, Ian. *Lost Paradise: The Exploration of the Pacific.* Topsfield, Mass.: Salem House Publishers, 1987.

Cook, James. *The Journals of Captain Cook.* Edited by J. C. Beaglehole. New York: Penguin, 2000.

Cordingly, David. *Under the Black Flag.* New York: Harcourt Brace, 1995.

D'Alleva, Anne. *Art of the Pacific Islands.* New York: Harry N. Abrams, 1998.

Denoon, Donald, et al. *Cambridge History of the Pacific Islanders.* Cambridge: Cambridge University Press, 1997.

Dodge, Ernest. *Beyond the Capes: Pacific Exploration from Cook to the* Challenger *(1776–1877).* Boston: Little, Brown, 1971.

Dudden, Arthur Power. *The American Pacific: From the China Trade to the Present.* New York: Oxford University Press, 1992.

Dugard, Martin. *Farther Than Any Man: The Rise and Fall of James Cook.* New York: Washington Square Press, 2002.

Estensen, Miriam. *Discovery: The Quest for the Great South Land.* New York: St. Martin's Press, 1999.

Fisher, Steven. *A History of the Pacific Islands.* New York: Palgrave MacMillan, 2002.

Frost, Alan, and Jane Simpson, eds. *Pacific Empires.* Melbourne: University of Melbourne Press, 1999.

Gibbons, Ann. "The Peopling of the Pacific," *Science* 291, March 2, 2001: 1735–1737.

Heyerdal, Thor. *Kon-Tiki: Across the Pacific by Raft.* New York: Washington Square Press, 1995.

Horwitz, Tony. *Blue Latitudes: Boldly Going Where Captain Cook Has Gone Before.* New York: Henry Holt, 2002.

Hough, Richard. *Captain Bligh and Mister Christian: The Men and the Mutiny.* Annapolis: United States Naval Institute, 2000.

Irwin, Geoffrey. *The Prehistoric Exploration and Colonization of the Pacific.* Cambridge: Cambridge University Press, 1992.

Kirch, Patrick. *On the Road of the Winds: An Archeological History of the Pacific Islands Before European Contact.* Berkeley: University of California Press, 2002.

Lamb, Jonathan. *Preserving the Self in the South Seas, 1680–1840.* Chicago: University of Chicago Press, 2001.

Lamb, Jonathan, Vanessa Smith, and Nicholas Thomas, eds. *Exploration and Exchange, 1680–1900: A South Seas Anthology.* Chicago: University of Chicago Press, 2000.

Levathes, Louise. *When China Ruled the Seas.* Oxford: Oxford University Press, 1996.

Lincoln, Margarette, ed. *Science and Exploration in the Pacific: European Voyages to the Southern Ocean in the Eighteenth Century.* Rochester, N.Y.: Boydell and Brewer, 2001.

Mawer, Granville Allen. *Ahab's Trade: The Saga of South Seas Whaling.* New York: St. Martin's Press, 2000.

Monmonier, Mark. *Drawing the Line: Tales of Maps and Cartocontroversy.* New York: Henry Holt, 1995.

O'Brian, Patrick. *Joseph Banks: A Life.* Chicago: University of Chicago Press, 1997.

Obeyesekere, Ganath. *The Apotheosis of Captain Cook: European Mythmaking in the Pacific.* Princeton: Princeton University Press, 1992.

Parry, J. H. *Trade and Dominion: The European Overseas Empires in the Eighteenth Century.* London: Weidenfeld and Nicolson, 1971.

Rennie, Neil. *Far-Fetched Facts: The Literature of Travel and the Idea of the South Seas.* Oxford: Oxford University Press, 1999.

Sahlins, Marshall. *How "Natives" Think: About Captain Cook, for Example.* Chicago: University of Chicago Press, 1995.

Sahlins, Marshall. *Islands of History.* Chicago: University of Chicago Press, 1987.

Salmond, Anne. *The Trial of the Cannibal Dog: The Remarkable Story of Captain Cook's Encounters in the South Seas.* New Haven, Conn.: Yale University Press, 2003.

Severin, Tim. *In Search of Moby Dick: The Quest for the White Whale.* New York: Basic Books, 2000.

Sherry, Frank. *Pacific Passions: The European Struggle for Power in the Great Ocean in the Age of Exploration.* New York: William Morrow, 1994.

Smith, Bernard. *Imagining the Pacific: In the Wake of the Cook Voyages.* New Haven, Conn.: Yale University Press, 1992.

Souhami, Diana. *Selkirk's Island: The True and Strange Adventures of the Real Robinson Crusoe.* London: Weidenfeld and Nicolson, 2001.

Thomas, Nicholas. *Cook: The Extraordinary Voyages of Captain James Cook.* New York: Walker & Company, 2003.

Williams, Glyn. *The Great South Seas: English Voyages and Encounters, 1570–1750.* New Haven, Conn.: Yale University Press, 1997.

Williams, Glyn. *Voyages of Delusion: The Search for the Northwest Passage in the Age of Reason.* New York: HarperCollins, 2002.

Williams, Glyn, and Alan Frost. *Terra Australis to Australia.* Oxford: Oxford University Press, 1988.

FICTION

Defoe, Daniel. *Robinson Crusoe.* New York: Modern Library Classics/Random House, 2001.

Edge, Arabella. *The Company: The Story of a Murderer.* New York: Washington Square Press, 2003.

Flood, Bo, with Beret Strong and William Flood. *Pacific Legends: Tales from Micronesia, Melanesia, Polynesia, and Australia.* Honolulu: Bess Press, 1999.

Hesse, Karen. *Stowaway.* New York: Aladdin Library, 2002.

Melville, Herman. *Moby Dick.* New York: Bantam Classics, 1981.

Melville, Herman. *Omoo.* New York: Dover, 2000.

Melville, Herman. *Typee: A Peep at Polynesian Life.* New York: Penguin, 1996.

Michener, James. *Hawaii.* New York: Fawcett, 1976.

Michener, James. *Tales of the South Pacific.* New York: Fawcett, 1989.

Stevenson, Robert Louis. *South Sea Tales.* Oxford: Oxford University Press, 1999.

VHS/DVD

The Discoverers (1994). Image Entertainment, VHS/DVD, 2000.

Explorers of the World: Ferdinand Magellan (2000). Schlesinger Media, VHS, 2000.

Florilegium: The Flowering of the Pacific (1984). Image Entertainment, DVD, 2002.

The Galleons (1996). The History Channel, VHS, 1996.

Kon-tiki: Across the Pacific by Raft (1951). Image Entertainment, DVD/VHS, 2001.

The Navigators: Pathfinders of the Pacific (1983). Documentary Educational Resources, VHS, 1982.

Sea Tales: The Final Voyage of Captain Cook (1997). New Video Group, VHS, 1997.

South Pacific Islands (1992). Questar, VHS, 1992.

The True Story of Mutiny on the Bounty (1997). New Video Group, VHS, 1997.

Wayfinders: A Pacific Odyssey (1999). PBS Home Video, VHS/DVD, 1999.

WEB SITES

Australian National University. "The Endeavour Project." Available online. URL: http://coombs. anu.edu.au/~cookproj/home.html. Downloaded February 26, 2004.

British Broadcasting Service. "Exploration: Captain Cook." URL: http://www.bbc.co.uk/history/ discovery/exploration/. Downloaded February 26, 2004.

Cowdisley Group. "The Bounty Game." URL: http://www.geocities.com/~jlhagan/A_Bounty_ Game/intro.htm. Downloaded February 26, 2004.

Discoverers Web. "The Pacific and Australia." URL: http://www.win.tue.nl/cs/fm/engels/discovery/ pacific.html. Downloaded February 26, 2004.

The Mariners Museum. "Age of Exploration." URL: http://www.mariner.org/age/index.html. Downloaded February 26, 2004.

National Library of Australia. "South Seas: Voyaging and Cross-Cultural Encounters in the Pacific, 1760–1800." URL: http://southseas.nla.gov.au/. Downloaded February 26, 2004.

National Maritime Museum. "Life at Sea in the Age of Sail." URL: http://www.nmm.ac.uk/site/ navId/00500300f008. Downloaded February 26, 2004.

The Natural History Museum. "Endeavour Botanical Illustrations." URL: http://flood.nhm.ac.uk/ cgi-bin/perth/cook/. Downloaded February 26, 2004.

The Natural History Museum. "The Virtual Endeavour." URL: http://www.nhm.ac.uk/museum/ tempexhib/voyages/endeavour.html. Downloaded February 26, 2004.

Polynesian Voyaging Society. "Polynesian Migrations." Available online. URL: http://leahi.kcc. hawaii.edu/org/pvs/L2migrations.html. Downloaded February 26, 2004.

Public Broadcasting System. "Crucible of Empire: The Spanish-American War." URL: http://www. pbs.org/crucible/. Downloaded February 26, 2004.

Public Broadcasting System. "Wayfinders: A Pacific Odyssey." URL: http://www.pbs.org/wayfinders/. Downloaded February 26, 2004.

Rice University. "Latitude: The Art and Science of Fifteenth Century Navigation." URL: http:// www.ruf.rice.edu/~feegi/index.html. Downloaded February 26, 2004

INDEX

Page numbers in *italics* indicate a photograph. Page numbers followed by *m* indicate maps. Page numbers followed by *g* indicate glossary entries. Page numbers in **boldface** indicate box features.